PARANORMAL COZY MYSTERY

Swords & Fallen Lords

TRIXIE SILVERTALE

Sittin' On A Goldmine
Productions L.L.C.

Sittin' On A Goldmine Productions, L.L.C.

info@sittinonagoldmine.co

www.sittinonagoldmine.co

Publisher's note: This is a work of fiction. Names, characters, places and incidents are products of the author's imagination or are used fictitiously and are not to be construed as real. Any resemblance to actual events, locales, organizations, or persons, living or dead, is entirely coincidental.

ISBN: 978-1-952739-07-1

Cover Design © Sittin' On A Goldmine Productions, L.L.C.

Trixie Silvertale
Swords and Fallen Lords: Paranormal Cozy Mystery : a novel /
by Trixie Silvertale — 1st ed.
[1. Paranormal Cozy Mystery — Fiction. 2. Cozy Mystery — Fiction. 3. Amateur Sleuths — Fiction. 4. Female Sleuth — Fiction. 5. Wit and Humor — Fiction.] 1. Title.

CHAPTER 1

"HEAR YE! HEAR YE! The 51st Annual Birch County Renaissance Faire is now declared open!"

A cannon fires and the crowd shouts, "Huzzah! Huzzah! Huzzah!" while they press through the gates.

As I gaze up at the Lord Mayor, of the Faire, and his goodwife pacing the ramparts above the gates to the Faire, I can't believe I let Erick talk me into this. Once upon a time, I simply admired Sheriff Too-Hot-To-Handle from a distance. But since we've moved things to the next phase, I have to be "open to new ideas" and other couple-y things.

Technically, I have nothing against the Renaissance Faire, aside from the way its supporters bandy about the letter "E" as though it alone possesses the power to travel through time. But before a frumpy old man with a bushy grey mustache showed up at the door of my studio apartment to deliver a message of inheritance and possibilities, I was living paycheck to paycheck, scratching out a meager existence as a barista in the woo-woo town of Sedona, Arizona. In my modern world, I didn't have the coin to engage in frivolous entertainment.

Since packing my one bag and skipping out on that monotonous existence, I traveled as far north as one can before officially entering Canada and discovered a wealth of—sorry to repeat myself—wealth and secrets.

I inherited a gorgeous bookshop from my late grandmother, Myrtle Isadora, and I discovered friends and, most importantly, family.

It was a shock and a thrill to learn that my father was alive and wanted a relationship with me. Losing my mother in a terrible accident when I was eleven left me an orphan, lost in the foster system for over six years. Wonderfully, the amazing discoveries in Pin Cherry Harbor didn't end with a family. My late grandmother turned out to be not quite as "late" as everyone assumed. Her hilarious and youthful ghost still resides in the bookshop, along with a spoiled-rotten and magnificent caracal.

Silas Willoughby, the man who delivered Ghost-ma's last will and a mysterious key to my hovel in Arizona, is an elderly attorney who also happens to be a highly skilled alchemist.

He and Grams devised a way to cheat death and tether her spirit to the bookshop, permanently trapping her on this side of the veil.

The most highly unexpected, but exciting, development has been my psychic powers. Grams had clairvoyant visions when she was alive and has even had a few since she took her ghostly form. However, my extrasensory perceptions come in all shapes and sizes.

"Mitzy. Mitzy, are you in there?" Erick's deep-blue eyes stare at me with concern and he rakes a hand through his golden-blond hair.

I smile self-consciously and try to cover up my dazed daydream with a tiny fib. "Oops. This place is a lot to take in. Maybe I got a little overwhelmed."

He chuckles. "Look, I'm a Ren Faire professional. Stick with me, and I'll make sure you don't miss a thing."

He scoops my hand into his and gives it a little squeeze.

I take a shallow breath, afraid that any sudden movement could wake me up from what I'm sure is a dream. Prior to this outing, I've enjoyed many a dream featuring our sexy local sheriff.

Erick tugs me through the gates with childlike eagerness. "First stop: turkey leggs and mead."

"Copy that."

"Why do you always say that?"

"You mean, instead of saying 10-4?"

He tips his head toward me. "Don't avoid the question."

"All right. Prepare yourself for a dose of truth, Erick Harper. I'm a film-school dropout."

He laughs and shakes his head.

"Seriously! I spent a good deal of time on sets as a production assistant, or PA. As a PA, one always has a radio with a headset and one must always be ready to do whatever is asked at the drop of a hat. To say that a PA is the bottom rung on the ladder would be an elevation of the title and an insult to ladders. So when instructions come over the radio from anyone above you in the chain of command, which is pretty much everyone, your job as a PA is to say 'copy that,' and then do whatever was asked as soon as possible."

"And that's why you dropped out?" He nods knowingly.

"What do you mean?"

"You don't exactly like following orders." Erick grins.

"Rude." After a quick pouty face, I continue, "No, I dropped out because I couldn't afford it."

"Oh, sorry. Sometimes I forget you haven't always been an heiress."

Punching him playfully on the shoulder, I declare, "Enough about my sordid past. Let's get 'ye old turkey legg' and you can explain to me why this is such an exciting local event."

"Once we get our supplies, it's straight to the jousting arena. The seats fill up fast, and we definitely want to be in the front row."

"Jousting? Like *Knight's Tale, King Arthur, Merlin* jousting? Is it all for show? It's not—"

Erick interrupts excitedly. "Oh, it's for real. I applied to be a knight when I was in high school, and I got unhorsed in the first round. It was fantastic."

Men. I'll never understand them. "Yeah, that sounds super fun." I surreptitiously roll my eyes as we queue up for poultry parts. Unfortunately, before we can acquire our sustenance, one of the realm's bawdy players accosts us.

"Oyez. I be Phlegm the Insultor. How much would ye pay for an insult on this day, milady?"

I have no idea what's happening, but I don't like it. I step away from Phlegm and shake my head.

"Come now, milady. Perchance you favor a sampling?"

Erick steps in front of me, protectively, and my heart pitter-patters. "Thanks, but she's not interested."

Phlegm is undeterred. "Perhaps a strapping lad

such as yourself requires a cut to thy quick as proof of my worth."

"Not today. Thanks." Erick turns away.

Phlegm puts a hand on Erick's arm. "Are you a lily-livered excuse for a man?"

With one hand, Erick grips the man's fingers and forcefully removes them from his arm. And with the other hand, he pulls out his badge. "In fact, I'm the sheriff of the realm. I'll ask you once to move along."

Phlegm's face turns almost as pale as my naturally bone-white hair, and he scurries off into the crowd.

My tummy flip-flops with a surge of admiration for my hero. "Thanks. Looks like I already have my own knight in shining armor."

Erick flicks his wallet closed and slips his badge back into his pocket as he smiles. "Let's hope I don't have to do that again today."

Clumsily offering a deep curtsy, I use my best old English accent, "Indeed, my lord."

With a turkey legg in one hand—and let me be clear, that's with a double "g" according to the sign —and a pint of mead in the other, we make our way to the jousting arena.

There are shops filled with handcrafted leather items, chain-mail jewelry, incense, spices, and Renaissance costumes, but it looks like shopping will have to wait until after the joust. Erick is practically sprinting toward the arena.

Unable to keep pace with him and prevent spillage of my mead, I stop and hastily gulp down half the glass.

Before I can set out to catch my disappearing knight, an attendee dressed as Robin Hood leaps onto a bench and shouts, "A wench after my own heart!"

I bow and hurry off in search of Erick.

The calls of the disappointed thief of Sherwood Forest follow me. "Come back! Come back, fair maiden!"

The arena is massive. I'm not sure exactly what I expected, but if it had been a circle of dirt surrounded by a few hay bales, I can't say it would've surprised me. However, this is a serious structure. Huge grandstands surround the arena on four sides, and there's a giant castle wall/rope climbing attraction on the back of the grandstand facing me.

Looks like fun, but I'm still searching for my date. When I round the corner, I stumble to a halt on the straw-covered dirt path and nearly choke on my recent bite of turkey legg.

Standing on the top of the fence surrounding the joust paddock, waving a blue and white flag, is none other than Erick Harper.

about the Queen gig. Not to mention, Twiggy works in my bookshop. Granted she's technically a volunteer employee, since she doesn't allow me to pay her but prefers to work for what she calls "the entertainment." But to keep a secret like this . . .

Queen Twiggy continues to explain the rules of the joust to the visitors, and I continue to stare open-mouthed.

Eventually, she completes her speech and moves under the shade of the overhang to take a seat in her ornately decorated chair. I suppose it's called a throne. Could this day get any stranger?

Erick grabs my hand excitedly. "Next is the Herald. He's hilarious."

"Who's Harold?"

"Not Harold, the Herald. The guy who announces the knights."

A man robed in red and black strides into the arena holding a large scroll, and, as if that alone is a signal that everyone understands, the crowd rises to their feet.

A thunderous uproar sweeps through the arena.

Stomp. Stomp. Clap.

Stomp. Stomp. Clap.

Stomp. Stomp. Clap.

The Herald leaps onto and over the fence, landing two benches to the left of us, and begins hyping up the crowd. "I am Sir John Jacob Jingleheimer Schmidt, and I, lords and ladies, shall warn ye of the dangers ye shall witness at this tournament. And whenever I go out, the happy people—"

The crowd roars to life, "There goes Sir John Jacob Jingleheimer Schmidt!"

He paces in front of each section of the bleachers, reading from his scroll, as he announces the knights in the first match. "Our knights in training, Sir Diddle Diddle and Sir Hickory Dickory, shall meet in the first match. Neither has fought in this land before this day, and only one shall emerge victorious."

Stomp. Stomp. Clap.
Stomp. Stomp. Clap.

Clearly, the traditions of the joust are beyond the scope of my understanding. But I'm a quick study. I'm sure you've heard things referred to as being so "punk rock." Well, it's more appropriate to refer to this joust as so "rock 'n' roll." It's what I imagine an eighties hair metal band concert would've been like.

The Herald sways to the cheers in the arena and jumps onto a bench right in front of us.

Erick gazes up with rapt admiration.

"In the second match, Sir Robin of Loxley, champion of the poorest, shall joust the Sheriff of Nottingham. Both hold many a tournament title, and today's battle shall preserve the honor of one man and send the other off with his tail between his legs." At this point, the Herald pulls a fox's tail from somewhere and wags it between his own legs—back to front.

The crowd roars with laughter.

The Ren Faire is a raucous group.

The Herald leaps to the top of the fence and walks it like an expert gymnast on a balance beam, as he sashays past the blue-and-white section. "And in the final battle, lords and ladies, the Black Knight—"

The whole crowd boos in unison.

"Fear not, good people. Your own Lord Mayor shall meet the Black Knight in combat this very day. And now, let us entertain ye!"

The horses charge through the gate one at a time.

"Sir Diddle Diddle!" A chestnut mare gallops around.

Cheers.

"Sir Hickory Dickory!" A muscular paint gallops out.

Cheers.

"Sir Robin Hood of Loxley!" Dust flies under the hooves of a roan.

Cheers.

"The Sheriff of Nottingham!" A massive grey stallion thunders around the arena.

Boos.

"The Black Knight!"

The crowd jumps to their feet and boos mercilessly as a gorgeous coal-black stallion with silky fetlocks gallops powerfully into the lists.

"The defender of the realm, protector of virginity—on weekdays at least—your Lord Mayor!" A pure white stallion with a glossy mane and a tail that nearly touches the ground bursts through the waving banners.

Stomp. Stomp. Clap.

Stomp. Stomp. Clap.

Stomp. Stomp. Clap.

The beautiful horses canter around the arena once more before disappearing through the gate.

Sirs Diddle and Hickory, if I was listening correctly, take their places at either end of the arena. Their squires step forward and hand them each a lance, a fair maiden drops a kerchief, and the horses launch toward one another.

It's utterly shocking how rapidly the steeds get up to speed. The lances ring out and Sir Diddle's shield is broken.

His side of the arena boos, while Sir Hickory's side of the arena cheers. After two more passes Sir Diddle emerges victorious, and Sir Hickory hunches over in pain as his horse canters out through the gate.

"That guy looks genuinely hurt. Is that part of the act?"

Erick's eyes are bright and his skin flushed. "It's no act. The joust is for real. On that last pass the lance slipped off the shield and rammed into his shoulder. I don't think he'll be jousting during the other two performances today."

I nod with mock sincerity. "Certainly not."

The Herald ignores the carnage. "Sir Robin and the Sheriff!"

Erick chuckles. "Sir Robin is an expert jouster. I hate to not root for the Sheriff, but he's got his work cut out for him."

As Erick predicted, Sir Robin of Loxley easily dispatches the Sheriff on the first pass. However, things turn in the Sheriff's favor when he knocks Robin's helmet off for two points in the second pass. The only way for Robin to win this last joust will be to unhorse the Sheriff. Or so I'm told by my super-nerdy date.

The horses launch into the attack and the crowd stomps their feet rapidly, creating a thunderous crescendo against the wooden bleachers.

The film-school student in me is thrilled with the diegetic sound. Sorry, once someone opens the gates to Nerdtown, I run through pretty quick. Diegetic means a noise that has an on-screen source.

There's a splintering of wood and a clash of metal as the Sheriff of Nottingham flips sollerets over helmet onto the ground.

The entire audience jumps to their feet and cheers.

The young girls running around the arena selling souvenir pennants have their work cut out, keeping up with demand for Sherwood Forest flags.

The Herald climbs up onto a bench once more. "I lear ye, good people of the realm, your champion!"

The beautiful white stallion gallops out from behind the gates, and the Lord Mayor sits in a full suit of gleaming armor with a long leather scabbard hanging from his left side. His horse prances around the arena as the crowd cheers and screams. He takes his position on the far right. The cheers transform to boos and hisses as the Black Knight emerges through the gates in a cloud of smoke.

Sweet special effect.

"The Black Knight!" cries the Herald.

"Boo! Hiss! Boo!"

The first pass goes to the Black Knight, and the crowd boos viciously. The second pass goes to the Black Knight as his lance splinters magnificently against the Lord Mayor's shield, and the crowd is going crazy.

The Herald climbs onto the fence and shouts,

"The only way for the Lord Mayor to save the realm is to unhorse this villain."

Stomp. Stomp. Clap.

Stomp. Stomp. Clap.

Stomp. Stomp. Clap.

The horses charge toward one another.

The Black Knight lowers his fresh lance.

The distance closes.

The Lord Mayor lowers his lance.

My bespelled mood ring turns to ice on the ring finger of my left hand, but my eyes are glued to the action and I can't be bothered with messages from the ether.

There's a deafening clash, and the Lord Mayor cries out as his body jolts backward and he flips off his horse. One foot is still caught in the stirrup as the massive white stallion drags the limp body of the Lord Mayor through the dirt.

The crowd is incensed.

As Erick leaps up, I finally look down and see the message in the glass dome of my ring.

A sharp metal spike tipped with blood.

Erick points to the Black Knight and cries out, "Stop him!" as he jumps over the fence and races toward the fallen Lord Mayor.

Unfortunately, I now understand the image my ring sent as a warning. The Lord Mayor is well and truly dead. This is no medieval play. This is murder in the here and now.

The Black Knight takes one look at the limp body of the Lord Mayor and charges his horse toward the opening in the fence.

Now, it's been a while since I attended equestrian summer camp, where I mucked out stalls and got riding lessons in the afternoon, but I do remember how easily horses spook. I grab a handful of flags from the souvenir girl's bucket, duck under the top rail of the fence, and run straight into the path of the escaping knight. I wave the flags furiously. Whether I'm lucky or stupid will be decided in about three seconds.

The black stallion puts on his all-hoof brakes, and the Black Knight launches over the beast's proud head. The metal-clad man flies through the air and lands, hard, on his back at my feet. The impact knocks the wind out of him and gives me time to scrape the sword out of his scabbard and hold it to his neck like Xena, Warrior Princess. "Don't move, brigand."

The line is a bit theatrical, I agree. But what would you say if you were to wield a knight's own sword and press it to his neck?

Paramedics are rushing to disentangle the Lord Mayor as Erick frantically searches the bleachers.

Without removing the sword from the Black

Knight's throat or my foot from his chest, I call out, "Erick! Over here."

He turns toward the sound and his face is awash with shock, admiration, and just a touch of amusement. Sprinting across the arena, he bends and pulls off the Black Knight's helmet.

I grin smugly down at the defeated murderer.

Erick's expression melts into dismay. "Grant?"

CHAPTER 2

THE BLACK KNIGHT strains to take a breath under the weight of my foot. I realize I'm more than a slip of a girl, but I find his monumental struggle mildly offensive.

He smiles sheepishly. "Hey, Ricky. Whatcha been up to?"

Ricky? I'd almost forgotten the adorable pet name that Erick's mother has for him. I don't need my extra senses to safely assume that Grant must be a childhood friend.

Before I can confirm my suspicions, the ever-round, ever-formidable Deputy Paulsen strolls into the arena with one hand on her gun. "Did she kill another one, Sheriff? The grandstands musta been full of eyewitnesses. I guess we'll finally be able to get her off the streets."

Paulsen slips her handcuffs from her belt and eagerly approaches.

Erick gently takes the sword from my hand and nods with his head for me to step away from the metal menace. "Paulsen, read him his rights."

The disappointment on Deputy Paulsen's face is palpable.

As she attempts to handcuff her quarry, I can't help myself. "Looks like I caught another one for ya, Pauly." Just to be clear, that isn't a nickname. Her actual name is Pauly Paulsen. But girls named Mizithra . . . Pot/kettle. You know the saying.

"Don't get too full of yourself, Moon. As far as I'm concerned, anyone who's had a hand on a sword is still a suspected accomplice."

The remaining knights of the joust approach. I want to point out that each and every one of them has a sword in their sheath. And that's not a euphemism. They legitimately have swords.

I gesture to the advancing army. "Looks like that's gonna be a real long list, Paulsen."

Scoffing under my breath as I walk away from the arrest, I carefully approach the Black Knight's stallion. "Sorry to scare you back there, buddy. Nothing personal. I just really needed you to stop."

The horse whinnies and I can't help but chuckle. Part of me was hoping I would be able to understand him, like I can understand Grams' entitled feline Pyewacket, but no such luck. However, he doesn't resist me gripping his bridle and leading him toward the waiting squire.

To the average spectator, I'm sure all the squires look the same. Having spent a number of years scraping by in the service industry, I'm all too familiar with the way people ignore and under appreciate blue-collar workers.

I'm not sure if my past experience influences my observation, or if my recollection is being aided by a soupçon of clairvoyance, but this is not the Black Knight's squire. "Where's the Black Knight's squire?"

The young lad's pimply face fills with genuine surprise that I noticed a difference. "Do you know Justin?" he asks.

"Justin is the Black Knight's squire? And you're, I mean, you *were* the Lord Mayor's squire?"

"Um, whatever. I guess I'm Butch's squire, but when he called in sick this morning the Lord Mayor stepped in so we wouldn't have to cancel the joust."

"Don't you have understudies? Like, other knights ready to step in?"

His scrawny shoulders shrug. "Sign-ups were low this year, and two guys got injured opening weekend. The audience expects the final match to be, like, two of the top knights. Without Butch here to play Lancelot, the biggest hype is for sure the Lord Mayor."

"How long have you worked the Faire?"

"This is, like, my second summer."

"How well do you know Grant?"

The boy's eyes widen. "You know Grant?"

When in doubt lie it out. "Sure. Him and Sheriff Harper grew up together." I'm spitballing here, so I hope my psychic message didn't mislead me. "Seems like Grant's a pretty big deal around here?"

The guy nods and mumbles guttural sounds of admiration. "Nobody can beat him."

"But isn't he destined to lose? Doesn't the crowd want good to triumph over evil?"

"Sure. Sheeple want a show. But we all know Grant is taking a fall. He choreographs all the battles and he invented the un-horsing flip. He, like, broke three ribs and a collarbone over the two years he worked on the trick, but now he can teach anyone. The audience loves the stunts."

"So why would he kill the Lord Mayor?"

The lad steps back and shakes his head in horror. "He wouldn't. Like, Grant takes the chivalry thing seriously. He would never dishonor the knights."

I hate to break it to this kid, but an arena jampacked with spectators just witnessed him do the most dishonorable thing I can imagine. "Then why would Grant tip his lance?"

The boy's brown eyes dart to the shattered lance lying in the dirt. "What do you mean?"

"His weapon had an iron spike on the tip, instead of the required blunt end. That's what killed the Lord Mayor."

"No way."

"Way. Where's the Black Knight's squire? I need to ask him about the lance."

He swivels his head to and fro. "I don't see him. He works the Jacob's Ladder attraction in between jousts. Maybe he's over there."

"Thanks for your help. I hope you get to be a knight next year."

"Thanks, dude. Me too."

Erick is inspecting the Black Knight's discarded lance, and I can see something dark red dripping from the point. My vision was, unfortunately, all too accurate. As I walk toward him, the final joust replays via my enhanced psychic senses and my stomach swirls. There's a flare of icy warning on my finger, but in the vision I can't see a spike on the Black Knight's lance.

Impossible.

Something draws me to the run. As I walk along the wooden railing which separates the two charging knights, there's debris on the ground near the middle of the run, where the knights clashed.

I hurry toward it, stop, and stare motionless.

"What is it, Moon?"

I nearly jump out of my skin. My focus was so complete on the grey shards on the ground, I didn't hear Erick approach. Without answering him, I kneel, pick up one of the shards of grey glass, and pop it in my mouth.

Erick grabs my arm and yanks me to my feet. "What the heck are you doing? Spit that out immediately. That will lacerate your throat."

I open my mouth, reach in, and pull out a sticky grey blob, which I drop into Erick's outstretched palm.

His face scrunches up in disgust. "What the—"

"Sugar glass. A movie-industry staple. You know those scenes when someone gets a bottle smashed over their head or crashes through a plate glass window?"

He nods mutely.

"That's not real glass. It's something called 'sugar glass.' It can still be dangerous, but clearly not as dangerous as plate glass. A dome of sugar glass concealed the iron spike on the end of the Black Knight's lance. This was no accident, Erick. This was premeditated murder."

Erick makes his excuses, begs my forgiveness for

leaving our date early, and I'm happily abandoned at the Faire.

He thinks I'm anxious to explore shops and buy a proper costume for next year's Faire, but I have other, more devious plans.

Approaching the Jacob's Ladder attraction, I immediately recognize the Black Knight's squire. The urge to run in guns blazing, or, more appropriately, lances tilted, has to be pushed aside. Grams is always telling me that you get more flies with honey, so here goes nothing.

Wandering around the rope ladder and chewing on my finger, I say, "This looks super hard. Can you show me how to do it?" I kick out a hip, tilt my head down, and bat my eyelashes. Trust me, I'm nauseating myself, but the ruse works.

"No problem." The young man smirks as he swaggers toward me.

I note that his fake old English accent vanishes in his haste to impress.

The strapping lad turns to the dodgy contraption and plants his feet shoulder-width apart at the base of the rope ladder.

The ladder is tied in a single loop at the top and the bottom, and it stretches above the ground at approximately a forty-five-degree angle. I'm no geometry expert, but it's not completely flat and it's not straight up and down . . . Somewhere in between.

Each rung of the ladder is a sturdy piece of wood stretched between the two lengths of rope. The trick is to climb from the bottom rung to the top rung and ring the bell, while the unstable rope anchors twist back and forth.

Most people flip upside down on the first rung and fall into the hay below. My host carefully balances his weight and manages to climb all the way to the top, ring the bell, look over his shoulder, and wink, before taking a roll in the hay. No pun intended.

"Gosh, that was awesome. Can you teach me?" My attempt at a seductive grin leaves much to be desired, but it must be a slow day for this medieval carnival barker.

"No problem, babe."

He helps me get an opposite hand and foot situated on the ladder. Then he promises to hold the bottom rung stable while I ascend. Clearly, this gives him a front-row view of my backside as I climb the ladder, but I'm trying to win friends and influence people here.

He cheers me on as I cautiously work my way up the ladder, and as soon as I ring the bell, he lets go of the ropes.

The ladder immediately twists and I fall into the mass of straw beneath.

He jogs up and his black curls fall over his face as he bends to offer me a hand.

I blush, for real. I have literally no ability to *make* myself blush. As I take his hand. He pulls me up with surprising strength, and I trip on a hay bale and fall into his arms.

Let me assure you, Mitzy Moon is not pleased. But this flirty bimbo that needs information takes every opportunity to milk the situation. "Wow, that is definitely as hard as it looks. Thanks for showing me the ropes." Wink.

Now it's his turn to blush.

"Hey, aren't you the Black Knight's squire?"

He smiles. But my psychic senses pick up on his underlying anxiety, tinged with fear.

"Yeah, I'm his squire. He, like, relies on me. Ya know?"

"Oh, for sure. Do you handle everything? Like his armor and his weapons?"

My mark is eager to brag. "Yeah, I choose his sword, his axe, and I line up all his lances before the tilt."

"That's so much responsibility. You should be a knight." I'm so glad Erick can't see me now.

"Yeah, I'm in training. Probably be the Black Knight next year."

I don't even need my extra senses to know this is

a pile of horse poo. "I'll be sure to come back and give you a token to wear in the joust."

I'm clearly more woman than he can handle. He backs up a little and blushes so completely, I'm concerned for his safety.

"Where do you get all the lances?"

His body language changes abruptly, and I fear my acting skills have reached their limit.

"What's your deal? Why are you asking so many questions?"

"Just seems like an important job. I mean, do they make them here at the Faire or are they, like, shipped over from England?" I can only play dumb for so long. The sound of my own stupidity is making me gag, and it's definitely affecting my performance.

"I don't know anything about the lances. You'll have to ask the owners."

"Oh, that's cool. Who owns it, anyway?"

Backing away from me, he mumbles, "The Lord Mayor and some other guy." He straightens the rope and brushes the straw from his tunic. "I gotta get back to work."

So, the Lord Mayor had a partner. What if this partner is the Black Knight?

Time for Mitzy Moon to officially take the case.

CHAPTER 3

GUESS WHO NEEDS an audience with the Queen? When I ran away from my final foster home at seventeen, I had to take some pretty crap jobs to survive. I mean, at one point I even made dirt. Not even joking. I worked at a plant nursery and made train-car-sized containers of dirt. One batch at a time. I had a recipe with words like vermiculite and perlite, and the dirt had to be cooked . . . It was a whole *thing*. But having to prostrate myself before Queen Twiggy and beg for her insider assistance is going to be the lowest of lows.

I wisely fortify myself with a fresh mug of mead and a shepherd's pie before I take the plunge.

Patrons and "players" alike are friendly and helpful. I make my way through the maze of fanciful wooden structures, which house shops, food vendors, and entertainers, across the fairgrounds toward the area where I'm told the Queen holds court. As I approach, a lavishly decorated barge floats downriver. Metal poles protrude from all four corners of the canopy, displaying banners in the colors of the Royal Court. The Queen, the court, and a small retinue of her guard are on board.

Boy, oh boy! There will literally be no living with Twiggy after this day. I take my place in line among the attendees queuing up for their personal audiences with the Queen.

The scow is a good distance upstream and moving slowly. If the human almanac behind me is to be believed, the river is especially depleted this year and flow is at an all-time low. He remembers the Queen's arrival in 1997, when two of her guards had to leap into the river and physically turn the barge against the current to avoid missing the landing altogether.

I'm not sure if you've ever seen a man in armor jump into a river, but I can't imagine it would end as well as he describes. However, legends like the one told by the human almanac are what make a Faire like this so—legendary.

It surprises me to see how many attendees are dressed for the occasion. The costumes vary from the subtle addition of a plumed hat above a T-shirt and jeans, to complete ensembles richly accented from head to toe.

One woman's getup is so cumbersomely adorned that she struggles to move. Her underdress is crimson silk with a gold and silver brocade corset-like contraption cinched tightly over the gown. Her hat is trimmed in sable, and beads of sweat trickle down the back of her neck. Her loud voice and bawdy commentary are at odds with the high station of her garb.

It's impossible to miss the one connecting theme between all price ranges of costume—ample amounts of cleavage. Regardless of peasant or nobility, each woman's bodice runneth over.

The flat-bottomed boat eases into its mooring and the Queen's servants tie it off securely. Her guards march off first and form an aisle for the royal procession. Various noble couples disembark and march through the procession, nodding and tossing out a "well met" here and a "well met" there.

A trumpeter steps forward and unfurls a purple pennant from the neck of his fanfare instrument. He blasts out a triumphant announcement of the Queen's imminent appearance, while a man dressed wig-to-boots in emerald-green velvet and gold brocade prances forward. With a dramatic gesture he declares, "Lords and ladies, prithee, give your attention! Queen Elizabeth!" He rolls his hand forward as he bows and steps to the sideline.

The moment we've all been waiting for, but none more than me: Queen "Twiggy" Elizabeth strides from her transport.

At this distance, I can see the fine details on her enormous gown—layers of purple silk, satin, and velvet, trimmed with fine golden embroidery. She even has a gorgeous cloak edged in faux ermine. Fortunately, the temperatures are reasonable and the humidity is low, so she won't overheat in that apparatus. Humidity is something I never talked about in the Southwest. Down there it's all about "dry heat," which, of course, is akin to being inside an oven. However, as I mentioned, the humidity is low, and the sky is a beautiful light blue, rippled with ribbons of thin cirrus clouds. See, Mrs. Manion, I was listening to your fifth-grade weather lecture.

Twiggy's regal air and haughty expression crack for a split second when she sees me waiting in the line.

I would literally give anything to hear her signature cackle right now and watch the shocked expressions on the faces of the personages of her realm. No such luck.

Twiggy glides to her throne, turns and addresses her admirers. "Good people of the realm, your Queen will now hear your concerns."

The crowd chants, "God save the Queen! God save the Queen! God save the Queen!"

As I wait for my turn with her Royal Highness, I amuse myself with some good old-fashioned people-watching. Many patrons have opted for the turkey legg. And I notice a common occurrence among the noshers. Their first three to five bites seem blissfully joyous, but once that initial layer of delicious meat is removed, an inordinate number of tough cords are exposed.

Chuckling to myself, I wonder if these turkey leggs are imported from some strange Jurassic-park-style farming operation. I've never seen that many tough elastic strands on a turkey leg anywhere else in the world. It's truly shocking. Very few people continue to gnaw at their turkey legg upon uncovering these unwieldy fibers. An unfortunate number of sinew-wrapped thighbones are chucked into the nearest waste bin. Maybe the extra "g" is for li-g-ament.

Alas, the moment of my audience is upon me.

Approaching the throne, I stop and curtsy, as I've witnessed so many of my predecessors do.

Twiggy's unmistakable smirk catches the corner of her mouth and her perfect old English falters. "Your Queen is listening, doll."

Straightening up, I cover my grin with one hand to avoid drawing any admonishment from the Queen's court. "Your Royal Highness, I would most appreciate a job in your realm. Recent events—" I raise my eyebrows and tilt my head in the direction I hope is toward the jousting arena "—require my assistance. Any task you assign would be most appreciated."

Twiggy has always been pretty quick on the uptake. As Queen, her intelligence is buoyed by her status. She turns to a woman in her court. "Lady Natalia, did you not just this morn inform me that your girl left and failed to give notice?"

The raven-haired Lady Natalia dips her knee in a small curtsy. "Yes, my Queen. I would be happy to employ this lass immediately."

Twiggy turns back to me and surreptitiously winks. "You shall find an appropriate costume at the Pendragon Tailor and then report to Lady Natalia's pickle stand."

I'm in the middle of bowing my head in thanks when I hear "pickle stand." My head pops up in time to see Twiggy snickering behind her gold-embroidered glove. I roll my eyes and shake my head. "My humble thanks, Your Majesty."

As I leave the Royal Court, Lady Natalia catches up to me. "I hope you were serious. I do need the help." She smooths her burgundy velvet

skirt and adjusts the golden cap adorning her intricately curled hair as she catches her breath. "I know
it sounds strange, but it's a popular stand, and this
girl just walked out this morning. No explanation.
I'd say you could wear her costume, but she took it
with her. I'm sure I'll never see it again."

Lady Natalia is high energy, and her statements
come with the rapid fire of a Tommy gun. I can
barely keep up.

"It's no problem. I'll run over to Pendragon's
and get a costume. I'm just thankful for the work."
The ring of truth in my reply even convinces me I
need the job.

A warm smile brightens her face as she nods.
"Thanks. You're a lifesaver. Ask for Chip at Pendragon's. He'll get you the right dress and he'll show
you the ropes. He knows everything about the Faire
—break times, employee restrooms, all of it. He's the
best. Thanks again! I gotta get back to the court.
There's nothing like being on the wrong side of
Queen Elizabeth!"

She doesn't need to convince me.

Grabbing a discarded map off the dirt-and-grass
pathway, I navigate toward the tailor's. However, I
make a couple of serendipitous wrong turns.

I stumble upon an incredible mask boutique.
The walls are covered with intricately designed
leather-and-feather masks. The colors and textures

take my breath away. Gold. Purple. Shimmering teal-blue. Peacock feathers. Strips of leather curled into fine tendrils that sway gracefully from the temple. Wow, just wow!

There's no resisting the pull. Plus, it only takes me seven seconds to justify the addition of a mask to my pickle-girl uniform. After all, I'm supposed to be undercover, and a distracting façade will certainly help me hide in plain sight.

My final selection is a contoured mask that covers both of my eyes and my nose, and angles sharply to hide the left half of my lower face. The leather is painted to transition from silver, through blue-green, to a satisfyingly deep purple at the jawline. Plumes of trimmed peacock feathers and black ostrich feathers adorn the brow, like a crown.

My next segue is purposeful. I have no intention of wearing a wig as part of this disguise, so a head covering of some kind will serve to hide my telltale bone-white locks. The proprietor is a sweet elderly woman who has been traveling the Faire circuit for over forty years and makes all the hats with her own two lovely, gnarled hands.

I buy five hats. I know, I'm a softy. I would've purchased ten, but she might've thought I was a psycho. It was hard enough to come up with a believable excuse for how my friends and I all like to dress alike . . . blah, blah, blah.

Anyhoo, five hats and one sumptuous mask later, I'm back on track.

Entering the large tailor's shop, I ask a young lady if Chip is available.

She disappears behind a muslin curtain.

A stout, barrel-chested man with a large waxed mustache approaches and bows so deeply that the huge plume on his cap nearly touches the floor. "How may I serve, milady?"

"Lady Natalia sent me. I need the right wardrobe to work at the pickle stand?"

His over-generous nature shrinks a fraction when he realizes I won't be buying any of the over-priced bustles or leather corsets. "Ah, a peasant's dress and perhaps a green bodice to accent your eyes and herald your profession."

Great, exactly what I was hoping for. A dress that screams pickles! Of course, I don't share my concerns, or the fact that my eyes are grey, with Chip. "Thanks. Do you take cards?"

"Why, yes. We take Master's Card and Mistress's Visa. The cards of the realm."

Despite his corny explanation, I am both shocked and happy. In my experience, the merchants in Pin Cherry Harbor are cash only. It seems to be the town that tech forgot. Even when plastic is accepted, the only device I've seen used is one of those old-fashioned credit card slidey machines. No chip readers here. But I'm in a place that exists beyond the time and space of Pin Cherry. Ye Olde Ren Faire. I wonder if Chip has a handy-dandy Renaissance jargon cheat sheet? I'm sure there's more to it than "ye" and "thy."

My session with Chip the tailor consists of him staring uncomfortably at every inch of my body as he instructs me to turn slowly. Creeptastic.

He marches into the back and retrieves a plain, tan muslin underdress, and a green overdress that laces at the bodice. Hanging both items in one of the ill-equipped dressing rooms, he waves me inside and pulls the crooked sheet closed. The thin cloth feels neither secure nor impenetrable.

Time to dig back into my youth and recover my ability to completely change clothes without ever technically being undressed.

Oh, it's quite a skill. One that, at one point, I was even able to duplicate while driving from one job to another. I won't bore you with the details, but it involves layering and a lot of intricate arm movements out of one thing into another, while slipping things out of neck holes . . . It's rather impressive.

Once I've completed my transformation, I peek out. "Chip, how does this work?" I point to the laces at the bodice.

He smiles with oily anticipation and ap-

proaches all too hastily. "You scoop up your nothings, and I'll lace you up."

Nothings? I realize I'm no Dolly Parton, but
they're not nothing. Rude. I scoop a hand under
each of my "cross-your-heart-encased" B-cups and
Chip reenacts the Frances Fisher/Kate Winslet
scene from *Titanic*.

When he's finished, not only can I not breathe,
but I can also rest my chin on my own—chest.

He steps back and raises both of his hands in
praise of his work. "Perfection."

"Actually, I can't breathe. You'll have to loosen
it. I'll never be able to handle pickles at this rate."

He guffaws and slaps the thigh of his pan-
taloons. "A saucy wench."

I had no intention of being *saucy*. But upon reviewing my comment, I can see where I went
wrong. "Indeed. But seriously, can you loosen this a
bit?"

Chip's entire gravity-defying mustache sags like
an abandoned marionette, but he obliges.

Looking down at my high tops, I shrug. "Do you
sell shoes?"

"You'll be wanting the Bard's Boots. Five doors
yonder and two shoppes from your pickle stand."

"Thank you."

Chip rings up my purchases and places my
mundane clothes in a bag.

I hurry down the row to find the leatherworker.

However, I'm once again distracted by a cart. This one offers elf ears for purchase. Not like disgusting "trophy" ears. They actually sell custom prosthetic ear tips.

How can I resist?

A tiny slip of a girl selects an "elven princess" design, fits them on my human ears, and color matches the latex to my skin with a few expert passes of her airbrush.

After the ears are glued in place, she holds up a mirror. "Thou dost bless the woodland," she says, with a bow of her head.

I'm starting to see the appeal of this Ren Faire counterculture. "Thank you. Can you direct me to the Bard's Boots?"

She wiggles her shoulders, which causes her fairy wings to ripple with life, and then flits across the tops of three bales of hay. At the end of the row she pauses and strikes a fanciful pose, pointing across the path to the shop I seek.

I bow my thanks and rush into the "shoppe" that promises to complete my ensemble with authentic footwear.

They have a lovely pair of suede ankle boots that I am assured are period correct. Not that I care, but I purchase the ankle boots and toss my high-tops into the sack with my other clothes.

The kindly leather merchants direct me to the pickle stand.

On the short walk to my new job, I pick a name for my Rennie character and secure my mask, careful to avoid disturbing my ears. Let's see . . . I know exactly two elves: Legolas and Arwen. I mean, I know the others, but those are the only two names I can access under pressure.

At the last moment I ditch the bonnet. I don't want to cover my ears, and I can probably pretend the white hair is a wig. Most people think that anyway!

Taking a deep breath to steady my nerves, I introduce myself to my new coworker. "Hi, I'm Arwen. Lady Natalia hired me about thirty minutes ago. How can I help?"

CHAPTER 4

THE TRAGEDY in the arena casts a dark shadow over the Faire, and attendance drops dramatically as the day wears on. Whispers and rumors rise. After a brisk couple of hours in the dill trade, my pickle pal —I'll trademark that—tells me to knock off early.

Still in full Renaissance regalia, I follow the thinning crowds out of the castle gates, into the huge dirt parking lot where, thankfully, the shuttle waits to carry me back to Pin Cherry Harbor.

Sitting on the cracked green-vinyl seat, I dig through my bag of mundane clothes and pull out my phone. Three missed calls from Erick and a pile of texts. I don't bother reading all of them. The theme is fairly consistent. He's so sorry he had to cut our date short and wonders if he can take me to dinner. Subsequent versions of the message reiterate the apology in increasingly more vulnerable ways. Since I'm not alone on the bus, I opt to reply via text. "On the shuttle. Should be back at the bookshop in twenty minutes or so. Myrtle's?"

As I move to drop my phone back in the bag—
PING.

"Yes. Where have you been? Went to the bookshop after I finished writing my report. It was locked up."

Chuckling, I won't even begin to try to explain my day via text. "Meet you at the diner in an hour. It's a lot to explain."

"Should I be concerned?"

"Aren't you always?"

Entering the bookshop through the heavy metal door on the alley side, it's strange to find all the lights off in the middle of the day. I walk across the first floor and stand at the bottom of the wrought-iron circular staircase that leads up to the Rare Books Loft. Some days I still find it hard to believe that my grandmother left all of this to me. A beautiful three-story bookstore filled with tales, and history, and magic.

My lawyer and mentor Silas Willoughby hates when I call it magic. He insists that he's an alchemist, not a wizard. But some of the things I've seen him do—

"Where have you been, dear? How did your date go with Erick? I've been frantic."

I shift my gaze from the tin-plated ceiling to the ghost of my late grandmother. Her elegant Marchesa silk-and-tulle gown billows around her as she floats down from the second-floor loft.

I'm the only person who can see and hear Ghost-ma, but the fiendish feline slinking his way down the stairs behind her seems to have his own inexplicable connection with her phantom form.

"Pyewacket, did you miss me?"

"Ree-ow." Soft but condescending. That's his equivalent of a cold shoulder. He sits back on his powerful tan haunches, licks one of his large paws, and cleans his black-tufted ear. His independent soul is never eager to admit any need for humans.

Grams zooms down to eye level, circles around me in a flash, and gasps. "What on earth are you wearing? And why do you smell like vinegar?"

"It's pickles. I'm running a pickle stand at the Renaissance Faire now."

She ghost-snorts and claps a ring-ensconced hand over her face.

"I'm serious, Grams."

"What the heck happened? Did something go wrong on your date?"

"I guess you could say it was *murder*."

Grams floats down and raises an eyebrow in

concern. "Oh dear, what happened? Did you have a fight?"

"Like I said, it was literally murder."

She stops so suddenly, it's as though I'm looking at a translucent portrait.

"Grams?"

"You killed him?"

Now it's my turn to laugh uproariously until I snort. "No! There was a murder at the Ren Faire."

"Oh, that's better."

"Not for the guy who got murdered."

"Mitzy! You're a corker!" She floats along beside me as I circle up the stairs and cross the thick carpets of the Rare Books Loft. Each of the individual oak tables holds a rare and valuable tome. Above each of the massive volumes is the green-glass shaded lamp, waiting to shed light on the past. Oddly, the pair of white gloves I'm used to seeing beside each book is missing. "Well, Monday is the research day, but Twiggy—"

"Grams." I point meaningfully to my lips. "For the seven-millionth time, we have a deal. If these pouty little babies aren't moving, you're not allowed to respond. No thought-dropping."

She mutely places her hands over her ears as though she is the "hear no evil" monkey from the classic trio.

I walk over to the candle sconce which serves as

the secret handle to my sliding bookcase door and pull it down, activating the mechanism that slides the bookcase back to reveal my swanky secret apartment. Stopping in the doorway, I turn to add, "Also, you might have mentioned Twiggy's side hustle."

Grams vanishes through the wall and meets me inside the apartment. "What's a side hustle, dear?"

I arch an eyebrow. "Queen Elizabeth."

Her ethereal eyes twinkle mischievously. "Some things have to be seen to be believed."

"I saw it. And I still don't believe it." Peeling off my Renaissance garb, I take my first deep breath in six hours. "No wonder women were always fainting. You can't get enough air to stay conscious in those contraptions."

"Fashion before function. In the perfect outfit, breathing is secondary."

One area where Grams and I consistently disagree is this concept of suffering for beauty. I'm all about function. I'd much rather be comfortable than couture.

"You wouldn't say that—"

"Grams!"

"Sorry, it's so hard to keep it all straight." She places her hands together in a "Namaste" gesture and gives me a floaty bow. "So, are you going to tell me about this murder that killed your date?"

"Good one. I see what you did there." Wincing

as I peel off my elf ears, I bring her up to speed. "Somebody tipped one of the lances at the joust with an actual metal spike, and the Lord Mayor was killed. Of course Erick had to make arrests and whatnot, so I entertained myself and obtained an audience with the Queen."

Grams eagerly zooms toward me. "Tell me everything."

I give her the CliffsNotes version of my request for employment and my day hocking pickles.

She is, of course, incredibly amused by my suffering.

"I've got to meet Erick at the diner. We'll talk more later. Maybe you can get started on the murder wall?"

She smiles so brightly, I swear she sparkles.

"I'm getting so much better at holding physical objects. I've been working on my memoir almost every day, up on the third floor of the museum. I can certainly write up some 3 x 5 cards for the murder wall. Enjoy your dinner and say 'hi' to Odell for me."

Tapping my lips with a finger, I hesitate before I mention our previous decision. "I know how much you miss him, Grams, but I thought we decided it would be too painful for him to know your spirit was trapped on this side of the veil with no way to talk to you."

As she takes in my reminder, her designer-gown-clad shoulders droop in a sadness that dims her otherworldly form. She floats slowly downward like a feather on the breeze. "I'm sure you're right. He's a good man. He was so kind to me at the end. We mended our fences and some days he made me forget I was even sick."

Staring at the ghost of my grandmother, I can't imagine her being ill. She was in her early sixties when she died, but her chosen "ghost age" is thirty-five. Her afterlife form is youthful and vibrant. I'm sure she was every bit the pistol Silas is always saying she was.

"Oh, I was."

Ignoring her breach of our agreement, I pull a hoodie over my "Never trust an atom. They make up everything" T-shirt and slip out of the bookshop before the emotions surrounding my precious relationship with Ghost-ma overwhelm me. Losing my mom in a tragic accident at eleven forced me to bury my feelings under an incredibly thick shell. As I bounced from one foster home to another—some good, most bad—I used sarcasm and silence to create a safe space around my heart. Nobody got in, and I didn't let anything out.

The free spirit that haunts my bookstore is teaching me to take emotional risks. I've actually allowed myself to love Grams, and my dad. I'm making room for strong friendships, too. But as I near the diner named after my professional divorcée grandmother, Myrtle Isadora Johnson Linder Duncan Willamet Rogers, I have to wonder if I'm destined to follow in her footsteps. Is Erick "the one," or is he doomed to be "the one right now?"

A brisk breeze sweeps up from the shores of the great lake nestled in our harbor, and I shiver as I grab the door and pull it open.

Odell peers through the red-Formica-trimmed orders-up window, gives me the standard spatula salute, and nods toward the corner booth.

Leafing through a small stack of papers, with his lovely blond bangs hanging down in a seductive swath across his face, is the man who makes my heart stutter and my tummy flip-flop.

As I slide into the booth, he looks up. It takes a moment for his deep thoughts to clear, but then his delightful blue eyes twinkle and he grins like a schoolboy. "You made it."

I shrug. "Well, I had to duck out early on the pickle stand, but I'm sure Odell will make it worth my while."

Erick leans back and snickers. "Pickle stand? Do I even want to know?"

Shaking my head, I grin and flash my eyebrows.

"I'm sure you'll want to know what your CI has been up to."

He puts a hand over his face and shakes his head in disbelief. "I never should've let you sign those confidential informant papers. You know that was a one-time thing, right?"

"I must not have read the fine print. Anyway, that's water under the boat—or dock—"

"Bridge?" He crosses his arms over his chest and it finally registers that he's still in civilian clothes. The short-sleeved shirt shows off his muscles in an irresistible way.

"Mitzy? You in there?"

Oops. Leave it to a film-school dropout like me to get lost in my mind movies at exactly the wrong time. "So, what's all this?"

He scoops up the papers, slides them under his left elbow, and leans across the table.

The gentle scent of woodsy-citrus wafts toward me and a hot chill coils around my spine.

"Tell you what, CI, if you tell me about this pickle-stand reference, I'll tell you about my papers."

I lean back and cross my arms. I want him to think I'm carefully weighing my options. In reality, I was about to lose control and kiss his handsome face. "How do I know those papers are worth it? I mean, those could be parking tickets for all I know."

He smiles. "True. True. But they're not." He runs his finger along the edge of the pages and fans them slowly. "These are copies of Grant's statement and the statement of Ursulina, Edmund Gurney's wife."

"Edmund Gurney?"

"The Lord Mayor."

My eyes widen with excitement and I hastily spill my Ren Faire story. I hurry through my audience with Twiggy and my fitting with Chip, but try to make my kosher dills sound exciting. "All right, now you." I reach for the sheets of paper.

Erick chuckles as he slides them out of reach. "You're seriously selling pickles?"

"I need to be accepted into the inner circle. Those Ren Faire folks are like carnies. They don't like outsiders. If I work there, I can make some headway and get some behind-the-scenes info. For instance, did you know that the Lord Mayor was a last-minute substitution? Some guy called Butch was supposed to battle the Black Knight, but he called in sick."

My extra senses pick up on his mild surprise, but he hides it well. "That's not significant. If this Butch was the intended target, then Grant wouldn't have killed Edmund."

"Wait, who? Oh, right. Can we agree to call him the Lord Mayor?"

Erick nods and slides the statements across the table.

As I skim through the information, Erick adds his commentary. "Grant is adamant that he's innocent. I went to grade school with the guy. It's not like we kept in touch, but he doesn't strike me as a killer, even though we both saw it happen."

"Yeah, and his squire is kind of an airhead. He doesn't seem like a murderer either."

"His squire?"

"What would you call it? It's squire, not page, right? The guy who hands him the lances." I lift one hand in a "how would I know" gesture.

"You talked to the guy? He was nowhere to be found when Deputy Paulsen was taking statements."

"He had to rush over to the Jacob's Ladder. He works two jobs at the Faire."

A grin tugs at one side of Erick's mouth, and he rubs a thumb along his stubbled jawline. "Not bad for an amateur. Maybe a pickle girl on the inside is exactly what we need."

I open my mouth to protest, and he bursts into laughter.

"Sorry, what did you say your alias was again?"

"It's Arwen to you, peasant!" The banter distracts me from the statements, but a surge of heat running through the band of my magicked mood ring pulls my focus back to the stack.

Odell places our plates on the table, and I inhale deeply.

"Best fries in Pin Cherry. Hands down." Reaching for my plate, I stop and stare at Erick's plate. Taco salad? He always has meatloaf and mashed potatoes. Before I can get the question out of my mouth, Odell has the answer.

"May to September is taco salad season for the sheriff."

Erick nods. "You don't win 'Best Mess' three years in a row and not know what your soldiers like to eat." He pops an official salute to Odell and digs into his chow.

Odell raps his knuckles twice on the table and saunters into the kitchen.

I admire the camaraderie that former soldiers share. Although Odell and Erick served decades apart, they have the unspoken bond formed from the common experience of time served in the Army. As I munch on my french-fried perfection, a smile touches my lips. Odell Johnson knows his customers better than they know themselves, and I'm grateful that he considers himself my surrogate grandfather.

Polishing off my burger in record time, I page

through Ursulina's statement as I finish my fries. "She's a trophy wife, huh?"

Erick stops midway to his mouth with a chunk of his salad's crispy tortilla bowl in his hand. "What makes you say that?"

"She's not much older than me. The Lord Mayor was in his early fifties, right?"

He nods. "He was in good shape, though. It's not easy to properly hold one of those lances on horseback. Jousting is tough."

"I guess you could say it's murder." I cover my mouth to avoid any food-related spillage as I chuckle heartily at my own joke.

For a moment Erick looks shocked, but his eyes sparkle with secret appreciation for my dark sense of humor. "You're terrible."

"Maybe. But I'm not wrong."

He leans back and exhales. "I don't know. She seemed genuinely heartbroken. Even Grant said that Ursulina and Edmund were 'seventeen and in love.'"

"So, they were faking it on their joint Instagram account and waiting for something better?"

His eyes widen. "Harsh." He leans forward and reaches for my hand. "Don't you believe in true love?"

Despite the tingling in my tummy, my inner

skeptic takes center stage. "I believe in truth and I'm on the fence about love."

A devious smirk turns up the corner of his mouth. "Duly noted."

I wait for my clairsentience, clairaudience, clairvoyance, or claircognizance to deliver some additional insight into that dubious comment—but no flash of information is forthcoming. "I'm not liking the sound of that."

He purposefully ignores my comment. "So what's your plan for the Faire, pickle girl?"

"Tomorrow, I hunt down the blacksmith."

"I'm bringing him in for questioning. You'll have to get in line."

"Don't look so smug, Sheriff. It's a solid lead. Maybe I'll poke around his forge while he's otherwise engaged." I finish off the last of my fries, wipe my mouth with a thin paper napkin, and slide toward the end of the bench seat.

"Try to stay out of trouble, okay?" Genuine concern flashes over Erick's features.

"I always *try* to stay out of trouble. My 'at bats' are just a little low."

Erick laughs until his face reddens. "You don't play sports, do you?"

I shrug noncommittally. "Why?"

"Just be careful at the Faire."

"Copy that." I bus my dishes and slip them into

the plastic tub behind the counter, wave to Odell, and wink at Erick as I leave.

If I'm going to complete a proper investigation of the Forge of Destiny tomorrow, I'm going to need some tips from the erudite Silas Willoughby.

CHAPTER 5

IN AN EFFORT TO practice my grandmother's famous "kindness rather than bitterness" approach, I put on my best manners when I call my solicitor. "Good evening, Mr. Willoughby. Could I interest you in perusing the selection of volumes Twiggy has pulled for the Rare Books research day?"

A rumbling sound of amusement followed by a gruff harrumph reaches my ear before he begrudgingly agrees to drop everything and come over to the Bell, Book & Candle.

"You have my eternal gratitude." Luckily, I end the call before I'm taken by a fit of giggles.

Grams rockets through the wall and nearly causes one of the pants accidents she's so secretly fond of inciting. "You shouldn't tease Silas. He's a powerful alchemist who could teach you more than any old book."

"If only! I wish he'd spend more time telling me about magic and less time correcting my manners."

"It's alchemy, not magic, and good manners make a person nice to know," recites Grams.

"Where'd you hear that?"

Her eyes search the ether for a moment. "I can't remember. It's funny how the paths are clouded, but the destinations remain clear."

Ever since Silas discovered a way to tether her spirit to the bookshop, Grams has been testing the boundaries of her powers. She can speak to me, and most likely Pye, she can see everyone, she has the rare posthumous psychic vision, and she can affect physical objects if she concentrates. In spite of all her accomplishments, she still can't leave the confines of this building, or keep certain pieces of her human memories from growing foggy. I hope she doesn't regret choosing to spend her afterlife with me.

A frantic ghost rushes toward me. "Regret? Never, ever, ever, Mizithra. You are the best thing that has ever happened to me and I'll never regret spending eternity with you!"

Her flood of love washes over me, but instead of joy a deep sadness hits me in the gut. "Not exactly an eternity."

Her creaseless brow attempts to furrow. "What do you mean?"

"When I die, I'll—"

A glimmering hand clamps over my mouth with surprising corporeal solidity. "Don't even say it!" Shimmering tears spring from Ghost-ma's eyes. "Silas will work something out. I just know he will. I can't lose you—"

I wrap my arms through the swirl of energy and cry like a toddler. "We'll be together forever?"

"Forever," she whispers into my hair.

A throat clears and the shuffling gait of alchemist-attorney Silas Willoughby grows louder as he intrudes on our private moment. "I will assume that Isadora is on the receiving end of that embrace and shares in your lament."

I sniffle and hastily wipe my eyes. "It's a long story."

Grams swoops toward her old friend and he shivers as she passes through.

"Good evening, Isadora." He reaches into the inner pocket of his well-worn tweed jacket and extracts a pair of wire-rimmed glasses. He hooks the gold arms behind his large ears and searches the air. As his gaze finds my resident ghost, his jowls lift with a warm smile. "You are looking every bit as lovely as I remember."

The spectacles have been worked over with

some alchemical mojo that allows Silas to see Grams. So, technically, I'm not the only human who can see her. I'm just the only human who can see her naturally. He can't hear her, though, but now that she's improved her writing skills, they are able to carry on a decent, although cumbersome, conversation.

He looks my way and the magicked lenses make his eyes appear enormous and round like a frog's. "I assume your summons has a purpose?" Silas smooths his bushy grey mustache with a thumb and forefinger.

The chuckle escapes before I can slap a hand over my mouth. "Yes, but you have to take those things off. I can't take you seriously with googly eyes."

After a lengthy exhale and an extra harrumph, he removes the glasses and eases them back into a hidden pocket. "Do you feel able to continue?"

I give a little sigh of my own and launch into the plan. "Tomorrow, I have to search the Forge of Destiny shoppe while Erick is questioning the blacksmith and I want to know if there are any powers you can teach me to help my investigation."

Silas snickers and his hang-dog cheeks bounce with amusement. "What is it that you think I may confer?"

Whenever he answers with a question, I've

learned that a lesson is not far behind. "Is there a spell for x-ray vision?"

As he takes a deep breath, my extrasensory perceptions pick up on strong disappointment.

I quickly right my wrong. "I meant alchemical thingy, not a spell." My attempt at an innocent smile falls flat.

"As I have elucidated on many occasions, alchemy is the careful and complex transmutation of matter. It is not magic. There are no spells. Your psychic senses combined with the principles of alchemy are a potent pairing."

"One time you said you could teach me how to read the energy of something. You said it was like forensics. Can you do that?"

He steeples his fingers and bounces his heavy chin on the tips of his pointers. "The question is, Mizithra, can you?"

And we're off. "I'll do my best."

He takes a seat in one of the chairs, slips his pocket watch out and hands it to me. "Close your eyes, hold the watch with both hands, and give me its provenance."

Lucky for me, I worked on a student film that fictionalized the authenticity of the Holy Grail and the word "provenance" was used several times in the terrible thirty-five-page script. For a short film that promised to trace the lineage of an ancient relic, it was as disappointing as it was inauthentic.

Back to the task at hand. I hold the gold watch with both hands and work to focus on the object.

"Release each fragment of information as it surfaces. Hold nothing back."

"You're not the first owner."

"Continue."

"The bezel has been replaced. It's not as old as the rest."

"Hmmmm."

My focus drifts as I wonder if the noise from Silas was confirmation or not.

"Keep trying, dear. You'll get better with practice."

Concentration cracks. "Grams! You can't whisper stuff to me."

Silas can't hear her side of the conversation, but he gets the gist. "Isadora, it would be best if you excuse yourself. I fear you only serve as a distraction."

If only he could hear her haughty scoff. I chuckle as she vanishes through the wall.

Adjusting my hold on the timepiece, I once again attempt to quiet my mental chatter and tune into the messages from the watch.

"It first belonged to your great-grandfather."

"Correct."

"But your grandfather gave it to you—for a

birthday—no, when you passed the bar."

"And?"

"His father gave it to him when he passed his bar." My eyes pop open. "Your grandfather was a lawyer too!"

A proud smile softens his face as his eyes drift off to a distant memory. "My great-grandfather and my grandfather were both barristers."

"Was I right about the bezel? Was it replaced?"

"Indeed, but why?"

Nothing ever comes easy with Silas Willoughby. I close my eyes and place one hand under the watch and one hand over—pressed against the glass face. A wave of fear washes over me and suddenly I'm not just receiving messages, I'm watching a movie from the point of view of—

"There's a fight. I'm protecting the workers. The cops are arresting . . . A billy club hits me in the gut. I'm on the ground. The fall cracks the glass. There's a gunshot . . ." My eyes rocket open. My skin is prickling with goosebumps and my heart is racing. The images feel real. What I witnessed didn't seem like the past. I drop into a chair, set the pocket watch on the table, and let my head fall into my hands. "What happened? What did I just see?"

"My great-grandfather represented the workers in the strikes for an eight-hour day in the late 1800s in Chicago. He helped organize a walkout on May

1, 1886. Unfortunately, the police came down hard on the strikers and violence ensued. My great-grandfather was beaten and arrested in the pursuit of justice."

"And I heard a gunshot."

"Sadly, some workers paid the ultimate price. It seems the greatest changes exact the greatest sacrifices."

"I'm exhausted. I feel like I ran a marathon."

"Energy must be exchanged. You will need to rest and recharge before this search of the forge."

I rake a hand through my messy hair and exhale. "Can I do this with anything."

"In a manner of speaking. However, objects that are blessed with regular use carry more energetic residue."

"Like your watch."

"To be sure." He nods and his jowls wobble. "Metal tends to preserve the potency for longer periods of time as well."

Rolling my eyes, I slouch back against the stiff wooden chair. "I have to search a blacksmith's entire shop—rapidly. I'm no expert smithy, but I'm pretty sure most of the stuff in there will be metal. How will I know which object to 'read?'"

"You will know." Silas smooths his mustache, returns his timepiece to his pocket, and shuffles out of the bookshop.

CHAPTER 6

THE GENTLE NOTES of a harpsichord seep into my lucid dream, and I enjoy a short waltz with Erick Harper before the alarm reaches a volume I can no longer ignore.

"Time to make the pickles." I scratch roughly between Pyewacket's tufted ears and wait for the deep thrum of his purr.

Silence.

"What's up, son? Are you having a pout?"

Pye rises up indignantly and drops something from his mouth to the duvet.

"Uh oh." I pick up the elaborate diamond ring, and whistle. "Have you been getting into a little 'cat burglary' while I was asleep? Where did you get this ring?"

He leaps off the bed, completely ignoring my query. "RE-ow." Feed me.

"Don't change the subject." I search the room and find no ghosts. "Grams! Grams, Pyewacket stole a diamond ring!"

In a flash, the distressed ghost of Myrtle Isadora blasts through the wall. "Is it a princess cut? I love a princess cut."

"I'm sure you do." I shake my head and point to the bed. "It's on the duvet. I have to get ready for my day of snooping at the Faire. Chip said the gates open at 10:00 a.m. and players are to arrive by 9:30. Since I think I'm a *player*—"

"That's my wedding ring!"

I whip my head back toward the ring. "Which one?"

Confusion swirls through her shimmering face. "What?"

"Well, Myrtle Isadora Johnson Linder Duncan Willamet Rogers, I was wondering which wedding that particular ring was from?"

"I'm not sure I like your implication, young lady." A bejewelled fist lands firmly on her round hip.

"What implication? You've had nearly as many husbands as Liz Taylor. I'm just trying to get some clarification, Missy."

Her fist slides off her hip as she chuckles. "Oh, I see."

"Say it walking, sister. I've got to wash my face and—"

"RE-ow." Feed me. Pye hunkers down and his tail flicks with irritation.

"Let me revise that. I need to head downstairs and pour some Fruity Puffs for my sweet baby. Is that what you wanted to hear, Pye?"

"Reow." Can confirm.

Grams trails along behind, focusing all her strength on gripping the ring.

I fill a bowl with my spoiled fur baby's favorite children's cereal and hurry back to the apartment.

Grams is still floating in my wake.

"Are you going to tell me about the ring?" I wash my face and attempt to lace myself into my Ren Faire wear.

"I can't remember." Her voice is barely a whisper.

Stopping with one boot on and one boot off, I gaze up at my grandmother's confused expression. "Here, give me the ring and I'll see if I can get a reading."

She moves her hand toward me, but quickly pulls it back. "No. No. That would be selfish. You need all your strength for the investigation. You can take a look at the ring when you get home. Maybe it'll come to me by then."

Tying the mask with a flourish and clumsily sticking the elf ears in place, I curtsy. "As you wish."

"Oh, Mitzy." The giggle distracts her for a moment.

"I'll see you tonight. Hopefully, I'll have some juicy gossip."

"Good luck, dear." Her words are encouraging, but the flickering of her form concerns me.

Hand-painted signs lead me to the employee parking lot and a special rear entrance for "Players and Merchants of the Realm." Since I am both, I stride through the gate with confidence.

The sight of Sheriff Harper and Deputy Paulsen leading an ox-shouldered man out in handcuffs knocks me down a peg. I duck behind a rack of wooden swords and thankfully avoid notice.

I don't need the help of my super-senses to confirm that the man in custody has to be the blacksmith.

Looks like the clock is ticking on my search. Time to rush over to the pickle cart, make my excuses, and get to the Forge of Destiny.

My pickle pal is very understanding when I describe my terrible "cramps." I promise to be back soon and walk away holding one hand on my stomach as I curve forward in pretend pain.

Not to brag, but I managed to get excused from more than one physical education class with this shtick.

The twists and turns of branching pathways at the Faire prove more convoluted than I remember from my one-day's worth of expertise. I have to beg a map from a shop before I'm able to find my way.

The Forge of Destiny is open and embers are glowing. Clearly, the blacksmith gets in early.

Wandering around the smithy, I wait for a little supernatural guidance.

Nothing. Nada. Bupkus.

Silas said that an item needs to be used regularly to leave a strong residue. I approach the anvil and pick up the blacksmith's hammer.

The second I touch the hefty wooden handle, my mood ring turns to ice on my hand.

Hooray. I'm on the right track.

I place my right hand on the metal hammerhead and continue to grip the handle in my left. Words begin to bubble into my consciousness.

Strength.

Swords.

Heat.

A woman.

A favor.

No. An exchange of favors.

I swallow uncomfortably, and silently beg the ethers to spare me the details of the exchange. All I really want to know is—

A feeling of power surges through my arms. I can feel the hammer striking iron.

A spike gleams in the light of a forge.

Water sizzles as the hot metal is plunged into a barrel of water.

"Hey, no one's supposed to be in—"

Shocked and weakened by my experience, I drop the heavy hammer and just miss my foot.

A slender young woman with a long blonde braid, twisted with red cord, hurries toward me. "Are you okay? Did you drop that on your toes?"

I lean on the anvil and take a deep breath to buy time. "I'm fine. Thank you." I paint my features with what I hope is the portrait of naïveté as I desperately grasp for a semi-believable story. "Lady Natalia sent me over here to fetch the pickle tongs she ordered. No one was around . . ."

A look of relief washes over the woman's face. "Oh, Simon had to . . . He'll be back later." She offers her hand. "I'm Ursulina. Let me see if I can find the tongs for you."

Crapballs. I didn't think this chick would actually look for my "little white lie" tongs.

"Here they are." She hands me a pair of perfectly formed pickle tongs.

I'm powerless to contain my laughter.

"What's so funny?" Her voice has a sharp edge.

"I never imagined myself picking up pickle tongs from a blacksmith. It's just been a weird couple of days, you know?"

Her eyes drop, her shoulders sag, and the gold circlet on her head slips off-center. "You don't have to tell me."

Maybe I'll push a little harder. "You seem to know your way around this shop. Do you work at the Forge of Destiny?"

She shakes her head sadly. "I'm part owner of the Faire."

"Oh, were you partners with the Lord Mayor?"

A hint of suspicion creases her brow, but she replies. "Edmund, the Lord Mayor, is—was—my husband. We were partners with Simon. I guess it's just me now." She draws a ragged breath.

I gently pat her shoulder. What is it that they always say in movies? "I'm so sorry for your loss. Maybe you should take the day off."

"I can't afford to." Her voice catches in her throat. "We're only here for seven weekends. I have to make sure we handle this PR nightmare and get attendance back up."

My ring confirms what the hairs tingling on the

back of my neck already suspected. Ursulina is the woman I saw when I touched the hammer. Despite her skill at playing the broken widow, she seems to be buttering her bread on both sides. "I have to get back to the cart. I'm here if you need anything, or if you just need to cry over a mug of mead."

She grips my arm as I withdraw my hand. "Thank you."

I smile weakly, and as I hurry back to the pickle palace the memory of her hollow remorse chills my blood.

By the time I return to the cart, my pickle pal, whose actual name is Joan, has amassed a line in the double digits. I immediately open the second barrel of pickles and help her serve the customers. When the next break in business comes, I show her my find. "I saw Lady Natalia this morning and she asked me to pick up these pickle tongs. Cool, right?"

Instead of gratitude or amazement, she laughs uncontrollably.

"I'm not sure what Lady Natalia actually meant for you to get, but those are not pickle tongs!" She doubles over as another fit of giggles seizes her.

"What do you mean? Look at the curved shape. It's perfect for picking up pickles." I was pretty pleased that my imaginary item actually existed, and I can't believe she's making a mockery of it.

"Those are V-jaw blacksmith's tongs. You better

get them back to the forge before Simon notices they're missing, or he will pitch a fit."

Note to self: Joan seems to have some knowledge of smithing, and it appears she is acquainted with Simon. No time like the present to win friends and influence people. I join in the laughter, at my own expense.

"When I ran into Ursulina at the forge, I thought she worked there. She must not know anything about smithing, though. She totally thought they were pickle tongs too."

This news sends Joan into another fit of giggles.

"How do you know so much about ironwork?"

"Simon's my brother. Well, half-brother, from my mom's first marriage. I'm the 'accident' from her second marriage. Before I was old enough to work at the Faire, I used to hang out around the forge with him and help with demonstrations."

"So, Simon is your brother?"

"Yeah, my half-brother. Why?" She rolls her eyes dramatically. "Let me guess, you have a crush on him?"

I chuckle uncomfortably. "Um, I think I saw the police escorting him out in handcuffs this morning. I'm sorry."

The color drains from Joan's face and she grips my arm. "Tall? Shoulders like a moose? Black hair, pulled back in a ponytail?"

I nod mutely.

"I told him to stay away from her." Joan mumbles this somewhat under her breath, but I'll take any opportunity I can get.

"Her? Who did you warn him about?"

She stands deathly still, and her normally sweet face hardens to stone. She spits a name out between clenched teeth. "Ursulina."

"The Lord Mayor's wife?"

She nods stiffly.

"Was he, you know, with her?"

Joan's angry expression instantly transforms into shock. "Simon? Having an affair with that that b—"

I slap a hand over her mouth before she offends the family of six lining up for pickles.

Attempting an old English accent, I smile broadly at the group. "How many pickles dost thou desire?"

The round belly of the father shakes with laughter as he holds up one hand, indicating five pickles.

"And five ye shall have." I retrieve the actual pickle tongs and individually wrap each juicy, kosher dill in a piece of wax paper before handing it to the mother who distributes them among the family. The youngest child throws himself onto the ground screaming something about "pickles" and "fairness."

His parents completely ignore him.

Struggling to keep my cheesy accent intact, I ask, "A pickle for the wee lad?" That definitely sounded more Scottish than old English. But clearly my sun-pinkened patrons don't notice.

"No. No. Number Three won't finish hers and Number One will only take one bite of his. In the end the little guy, Number Four, will get more pickles than all the rest."

At $3.50 per pickle, I respect the woman's effort to avoid wasting her dill dollars. I smile and nod. Something my mother always used to say, and despite the years that have passed since her death, I always remember. "If you don't have something nice to say, say nothing at all, but at least smile and nod so the person feels acknowledged."

The wailing, dirt-covered child has already picked himself up. And, as predicted, the older brother passes down his pickle and instantly starts begging his father for a wooden sword.

The wisdom of mothers. My mother didn't live long enough to see how much I would grow to appreciate her maternal instincts. As a little girl, I distinctly remember hating rules and sharing the tantrum-y lad's feelings about life not being fair. But once I lost my mother, I came to understand a new level of inequality in the world. And I would give anything to have her rules and lectures back in my life for just five minutes.

"Arwen? You did say your name was Arwen, right?"

I shake my head to dislodge the heartbreaking memories and force a smile that doesn't touch my eyes. "Yes, sorry Joan. That bratty kid must've distracted me."

"Right? Can you imagine having four of those rugrats screaming, shouting, and begging for souvenirs at the Faire? I wouldn't want to begin trying to foot the bill for that."

Desperate to turn the conversation back to Simon and find out what his connection is to Ursulina, I take one of my famous shots from left field. "So it's just you and your brother? Are your parents still alive?"

Joan tilts her head to the side and scrunches up her nose. "What a weird question. Of course my parents are still alive. Aren't yours?"

A cloud passes over my face and my pain is reflected in Joan's eyes.

She covers her mouth with her hand and shakes her head. "I'm so sorry. I'm such an idiot. People are always telling me I talk without thinking." She slaps the palm of her hand against her own forehead. "Such an idiot. Let's forget I even asked that stupid question. Let me answer yours instead. Simon has his own apartment, which he shares with a bunch of roommates. But he travels, like, a lot of weeks out of the year with the Faire, so he's not there much. I still live at home. Lame, I know. But my stepdad's actually super nice, and I have, like, the whole basement to myself."

My inner film-school dropout is desperate to write a scene imagining what my life would be like if my mother was still alive. I dig my fingernails into the palm of my own hand in an attempt to force myself to focus. "So if Simon wasn't involved with Ursulina, why did you warn him about her?"

Joan shakes her head and exhales. "She's trouble. This is only my second year working at the Faire, but the rumors about her " She stops abruptly. "I can't even."

Somehow, I'm going to have to figure out a way to convince her to "even" because I need some dirt. "Seriously? Like what kind of stuff?"

Joan gives me a conspiratorial side-eye as she whispers, "What you said about an affair isn't that far off. I've heard stories about her, you know, with a few different people."

I need something concrete. Joan is clearly a colossal gossip, but she doesn't appear to be that fussy about details. "Really? Do you think any of it's true?"

Joan stares at me like I must be crazy for asking. "What do you mean? Everyone's talking about it."

I'm starting to worry that Joan might not be a great source of information. She clearly likes to play pretty footloose and fancy-free with her facts. At least I can get some more information about Simon. "So how long has Simon been traveling with the Faire?"

"Only the last three years. He was an apprentice to the previous blacksmith for five years. Then he took over managing the Forge of Destiny for the Pin Cherry Harbor Renaissance Faire and one in another nearby state. But last year he saved up enough money to buy in on the whole operation."

"Wow. That's industrious. No wonder everyone has a crush on him."

Joan rolls her eyes. "Please don't start. I don't think I can—"

As she falls silent, a strange look seeps into her eyes and my skin tingles with the unmistakable sensation of fear.

Turning, I follow her gaze. A tall man in an executioner's hood is marching our way and carrying an enormous halberd. There are six or seven wild men dressed in the Renaissance version of a straightjacket, and I'm immediately reminded of "The Gentleman" episode of *Buffy the Vampire Slayer*. This guy gives off a decidedly horrifying vibe, and the deranged maniacs circling around him only serve to double down on the terror.

For a split second something trickles past the fear and horror, but it slips away like an eel in ice water as Joan mumbles her disgust.

"Bunch of freaky knaves. Makes my skin crawl."

As soon as the entourage passes, I grip her arm. "Who is that?"

"The Executioner."

"I gathered that. But I mean, who is it really? Like, who's the man behind the mask?"

Joan's voice is a frightened murmur. "No one knows. He's like Joaquin Phoenix. Totally method. He never takes off the hood."

The hairs on the back of my neck tingle and I shake my whole body to push the image away. "Creepy."

Pickle patrons, some in costume and some in their mundane clothes, consume the remainder of the day. Mundane is the term we Rennies use to refer to those folks who can't be bothered to dress for the Faire. I'm officially part of the inner circle. Yay me.

As I head toward the back gate at the end of my shift, I notice Ursulina in a heated discussion with the blacksmith.

Opportunity, I hear you knocking!

Circling back to the cart, I retrieve the tongs, slap on my dumb-blonde smile, and wander toward the pair. By the way, I can say dumb blonde because, technically, I am a blonde, even though I fall on the extremely light end of the spectrum. So, I'm reclaiming the concept for my kind.

As I approach the huddled conversation, I reach out with my extra senses. Ursulina is giving off a genuinely terrified vibe, and Simon's energy is kind of threatening.

"Hey, sorry to interrupt."

When Ursulina turns toward me, her eyes are red-rimmed and she hastily swats a tear from her cheek.

Simon's scowl softens for a moment, but when he sees the tongs in my hand his anger flares. "Where did you get those?"

Now's my chance to gain some favor with the Lord Mayor's widow by not throwing her under the bus. "I took them by mistake this morning. I thought they were pickle tongs. But your sister set me straight."

His energy immediately shifts and he smiles broadly, revealing the handsome swagger that must make all the girls swoon. "You work with Joanie?"

For some reason, all I can think of is *Happy Days* and Joanie and Chachi. I hand him the tongs and offer a passable Fonzie impression, "Heeeeey."

Simon's half grin oozes discomfort, but he takes the tongs.

My face reddens. It wouldn't be the first time my years of television babysitters have betrayed me. "So, yeah. I work with Joan. She told me I better give them back, or risk your wrath." My chuckle sounds phony to my own ears.

"No problem. Any friend of Joanie's is okay by me." He narrows his gaze and looks at me appraisingly. "You new? I don't remember seeing you at orientation."

This comment brings an accusing stare from Ursulina, and she crosses her arms over her burgeoning bust, right below an ostentatious ruby pendant. Based on her earlier cries of money woes, I'll assume it's as fake as her accent.

"Lady Natalia just hired me yesterday. I guess her other girl quit without notice, so she was in quite a bind, you know." The desperation in my voice makes my throat dry. However, the story seems to hold.

Simon and Ursulina exchange a glance that would escape most people. Luckily, my ring sizzles to life on my left hand and the mist in the stone swirls to reveal an image of the Lord Mayor. "Did you know her? The girl who quit?"

"She was new. Not the type I'd hire." Ursulina chews the inside of her cheek and avoids my gaze.

I'd love to ask who hired the girl, but my senses, the regular and the extras, are getting a real "cheating husband" vibe from Ursulina. "It was nice to meet you, Simon. Sorry about the tongs mix-up. I'll see you both next Saturday."

"I hope you mean Friday." Simon shrugs. "Next weekend is a three-day. It's Festival Friday."

"Oh, thanks. I wouldn't want to miss that." I'm getting pretty good at this undercover stuff. That fib even convinced me.

As I turn to leave, Ursulina grips my arm with surprising force. "You could stay for the after-party."

Looks like my "taking one for the team" earned a few brownie points with the widow. My curiosity burns, but I need to talk to Erick. Besides, if the legends are true, I'm a little too out of practice to roll with their after-hours debauchery.

The best lies are wrapped in a version of the truth. "Oh, I have to get home to take care of my grandmother. Maybe I can set something up for next weekend."

She pats my arm. "You're such a kind person."

I smile at them both and hurry out of the gate. Am I a kind person? This Arwen character I'm playing seems all right. Maybe I'm more thoughtful than I, well, thought.

CHAPTER 7

THE BRICKS of the three-story Bell, Book & Candle are warmed by a pink and violet sunset as I turn down the alley. All in all, it has been a pretty productive day.

Erick's text indicates he'll arrive by 7:00 p.m. and he promises to bring food. As if there aren't already enough reasons for my heart to race. A handsome man, with a job, who brings me food? Be still my beating heart!

BING. BONG. BING.

The bell at the alley door sounds and smacks me back to reality. I wasted valuable primping time, wandering around in my daydream.

Running to the alley door, I lean against it and call through. "Who is it?"

"It's your delivery from Red Door Szechuan, Miss."

Ooooh, that voice. I shove the heavy metal door open—

"Oh dear! You should have told me you had a date."

"Grams!" Oops. I said that out loud. Erick is staring at me like I'm straight-up crazy town. "I mean, that was Grams' favorite restaurant. How thoughtful."

He nods, but his eyes are full of suspicion.

A quick telepathic message to Grams should clear things up. *Now that you know that I have a date, can you please make your ghostly self scarce before Erick calls a nuthouse to have me committed?*

Of course. So sorry, dear.

"Did you want me to come in, or is this costume part of our alley picnic?" Erick runs a hand through his hair and an enticing swath of bangs drops over one eye.

My tummy flips and my arms flare with goosebumps. "Give me five minutes to change out of this getup, while you set up the grub in the back room. Just don't touch the Fruity Puffs. Pye will murder you on the spot."

"10-4, or what is it you always say? Copy that?" He grins and snickers.

Chuckling, I reply, "Yeah, copy that."

He brushes past me with a wink and sets the to-go bag down on the table. "No Fruity Puffs. Understood. Because, normally when I'm left unsupervised, the first thing I go for is the kid's cereal."

Putting a hand on my hip, I scowl. "Go ahead and joke. It's your funeral, copper."

I run up the wrought-iron circular staircase, and Grams accosts me as soon as I pull the candle handle next to my precious, recently recovered, *Saducismus Triumphatus.*

She flashes her eyebrows and wiggles her designer-gown clad shoulders. "So you want me to make myself scarce. Big plans?"

I roll my eyes as I strip off layers of historically accurate garb. "It's business."

"Do you mean monkey business?" She giggles uncontrollably.

"Oh brother. Seriously? You're worse than any of the immature girls that hung out in my posse back in Arizona. I'm a confidential informant for the Pin Cherry Harbor Sheriff's Department. I'm simply making my report."

Ghost-ma swirls around me, nodding patronizingly. "Mmhmm. Sure. Sure. I bet Sheriff-Too-Hot-To-Handle takes dinner to all his CIs."

A leather ankle boot takes flight as I huck the projectile in her general direction.

She squeals with delight and vanishes.

Taking advantage of her absence, I wiggle into my skinny jeans and pull on a tee with an image of a cartoon kitten skeleton and the phrase, "I'm Crazy On The Inside."

Accurate.

As I push the ornate plaster medallion that activates the bookcase door from inside the apartment, a soft thud connects with my head.

What the— I turn just in time to see my gleeful Ghost-ma vanish through the wall.

Picking up the bunny slipper as the door slides open, I toss it toward the general area where she disappeared. "I'll deal with you later."

I spin around to discover Erick standing at the top of the stairs with one eye squinting in concern. "Anything you want to tell me?"

Think. Think. Think. "Yes. Pyewacket was chewing on my shoe."

He crosses his arms over his tight-fitting blue T-shirt and nods.

I'm immediately lost in a little push-in dolly-shot of my own, as I pan across his inviting muscles and crooked smile.

"So, you have two cats. And both of them are named Pyewacket."

Uh oh. My throat tightens, and swallowing seems to be beyond my abilities. "What's that now?"

"Because I just fed half of a pork egg roll to a large tan caracal—downstairs. Ten seconds ago."

The pinkish hue creeping up my neck threatens to out me, so I dig into my bag of tricks and pull out my one failsafe measure.

A few rapid strides take me dangerously near and I lean against Erick's chest as I whisper, "Maybe I should be asking what you were doing sneaking up to my bedroom?"

Direct hit!

He blushes profusely, steps back, and has to grab the railing to keep from stumbling backward down the twisty steps.

While he's off balance, I swish by. "I hope there's an egg roll left for me."

His footsteps are right behind me. "And I grabbed your favorite."

Pausing with a deep-fried treat halfway to my mouth. "How do you know my favorite Chinese food?"

He shrugs. "That one time when I came by—to take a report or something—you were eating leftover sweet-and-sour chicken."

My heart swells, and I can almost hear the orchestral music follow. He knows my favorite Chinese food. He noticed. That's got to be one of the signs of true love.

"Was I right?" His big blue-grey eyes cloud with worry.

I take a bite of the egg roll, chew slowly, and swallow. "Yeah, you're right. But don't get cocky. I know stuff about you too."

He saunters to a chair and sits casually. "Enlighten me, Moon."

Oh, he's using my last name. It's definitely go time. "All right, Ricky, strap in."

He blushes adorably when I use his mother's pet name for him.

"Your favorite meal is meatloaf and gravy."

"Too easy." He loads a plate with rice and broccoli beef.

"You had a pot belly pig named Casserole."

His eyes widen. "Well remembered."

And then something happens that I can't explain. Images, sounds, and feelings flood through me. "You had a blue ten-speed bike with a denim seat. Your neighbor used to bake you Christmas cookies every year until she passed away three years ago. Your best friend in high school was named Brad. You played baseball for one season and ran track for three. You won the seventh-grade Science Fair. Your first car was a Gremlin. Your favorite movie is *Apocalypse Now*. You're afraid of spiders. You—"

A hand grips my arm and my body feels as

though it's being pulled from a rushing river. Slowly the flood of information recedes and I gasp for air.

"What are you playing at?" Erick's face is a mask of concern, tinted with suspicion. "Did Paulsen put you up to this?"

I'm not sure if my feminine wiles could save me now, even if I stripped naked. But maybe—

"Don't you dare, missy!" The furious warning of Grams shocks me to my senses—the regular ones.

I rub a hand across my face and take a deep breath, while I cook up a story. "Whew! That was crazy, right?"

"Crazy is one word for it." He pulls his hand back and fixes me with an expectant gaze.

"It's something I picked up back in Sedona. That place is the woo woo capital of the world, you know?" I circle a finger at my temple in the international sign for wackadoo. "I think it's called psychoscopy, or something? It's just reading the energy of things."

He nods slowly. "Okay. I'll buy that, I guess. But that was more than a parlor trick, Mitzy. You were dead on—with everything. I've worked with a so-called psychic or two on missing child cases, when parents get desperate. Their information is usually vague and unhelpful. But that . . . I don't know whether to be impressed or terrified."

A specter appears behind his head. "Careful,

sweetie. Don't blow it. You can push him toward 'impressed' if you're careful."

I rocket a secret thought-message at Grams. *You seriously have to get out of here. It's hard enough to maintain normal after what just happened. I can't start talking to ghosts—again.*

I'm sure you're right, dear.

I smile nonchalantly and load up a plate with fried rice and sweet-and-sour chicken. "I suppose you get better with practice."

"Mmhmm. So, about how often do you pull out your crystal ball, Madam Moon?"

I cackle wildly. "Oh, that's a good one." Sliding the box of crab wontons between us, I attempt an urgent subject change. "That last one's yours. Did I tell you what I found at the forge?"

He takes a bite and talks with his mouth a little full, which doesn't bother me in the least, since I would definitely be the pot and the kettle if I took any offense. "Not yet, but I gotta say I'm on the edge of my seat."

Ignoring his gibe at my previous display, I *forge* ahead with my report. See what I did there? "When I came into work this morning I saw you and Paulsen hauling that big fella out. I figured a guy with shoulders like that was either the blacksmith or a children's ride."

Erick shrugs his shoulders. "He's not that big."

I detect a hint of jealousy, but I'll let that lie. "So I told Joan— Not important. I went over to search the forge and I'm positive that he made the spike."

"Me too. But my confidence is based on Simon's sworn statement. How can you be so sure?"

Dagnabbit! I'm supposed to be pulling myself out of trouble not digging in deeper. "I overheard him arguing with Ursulina." Not an entirely true statement, but it's better than telling him I had a vision!

Erick leans forward. "He claims Ursulina commissioned the spike as a gift for the Lord Mayor's birthday."

"Geez! Remind me not to invite her to my party."

"Yeah. That's where the story gets fuzzy. He says that she asked for a replica of the finial from one of the Sultan of Demak's staves."

"What are you talking about?"

Erick nods. "Right, I forgot to tell you about Edmund—the Lord Mayor's—addiction."

"Young wenches?"

He stops and tilts his head. "Put a pin in that."

I pantomime pushing a tack into an invisible board while he continues.

"Ursulina claims that he had an obsession for Renaissance and Renaissance-adjacent junk. He would scour online auction sites and flea markets for anything that looked old and knight-ish. Her word, not mine. So she wanted Simon to create a replica of this particular finial, one called Pecruksili, for her husband's collection."

"And he did? He made the murder weapon?"

"Technically, yes. But Simon swears he had no idea she intended to use it to murder Edmund."

"What makes you think she was involved in murdering him? It's not like she was wielding the lance."

Erick tilts his head and raises one hand. "Come on. She ordered the thing. Plus, if we go back to that pin I told you to put in the 'wenches' thing, the Lord Mayor was known to be quite a gadabout."

I can't stop myself from a guffaw. "Gadabout? Don't you mean sleazy lech? The previous girl who worked at the pickle stand quit because of his unwelcome advances."

"And when exactly did you question her?"

"No, Ursulina was crying. Girls know stuff, all right?" I don't care for his bemused expression. "Not to mention, if Ursulina picked up the finial, how did it get onto the Black Knight's lance?"

Erick sighs, his hands fall into his lap and he leans back. "Welcome to the stall in my investigation."

"Don't worry. If you can't catch a break in the

case this week, I've been invited to the after-party next weekend."

His jaw clenches. "By who?"

"I think you mean, 'by whom' and, if you must know, it was Ursulina."

He shakes his head, and his eyes search through an invisible register of facts. "Her husband was murdered yesterday, she's a prime suspect, and she's still planning on going to an after-party?"

"What's your point?"

He looks up and fixes me with a look that screams: "You can't be serious?"

"JK. JK. I get it. It's pretty shady to be out partying that soon, but if this guy was cheating on her all the time . . . Maybe she was—"

"Happy to have him out of the way?" Erick interjects.

"Yeah. That doesn't look good." I slouch into my chair and chew on the inside of my cheek.

A crash from somewhere in the bookshop startles me out of my silent analysis of the facts.

Erick is out of his chair in a flash and motions for me to keep quiet. "Stay here," he whispers.

Has he met me?

I creep along behind him as quietly as possible, matching his semi-crouched position.

He looks back, opens his mouth, rolls his eyes, and continues.

As we make a right turn into the stacks, I'm unsurprised to see Pyewacket casually cleaning his left ear, awash in the faltering sunlight filtering through the 6 x 6 front windows and illuminating the drifting dust motes.

Erick's shoulders visibly relax and he kneels to retrieve the tumbled tome.

"Here, let me see that." I reach toward the book.

He turns and jokes, "I may not be a librarian, but I can probably figure out where it goes."

"It's not that. Normally, when Pye knocks books off the shelves, it tends to be for a reason."

Erick slowly hands me the book, as his perfectly pouty lips pinch together in thought. "First, you're talking to imaginary cats, then it's a quick game of psychoscopy, and now your cat is communicating with you through fallen books?"

He's not wrong. Before answering, I grab the particular book that Pyewacket selected from Erick's outstretched hand and read the title aloud. "*Famous Weapons Throughout the Ages.*" I kick out one hip and put my fist on it as I add, "You have to admit, it's an interesting selection based on our current investigation of reproduction finials."

"Re-ow." Thank you.

"You're welcome, and message received, Pye. You can go back to your very important napping."

"Ree-ow." Soft but condescending.

"I don't appreciate the tone, mister."

Erick's eyes track back and forth between me and my fiendish feline until finally he comments, "So, you're having a conversation with a cat right now?"

"Look, Harper, don't pretend like you and your precious potbelly pig never had a little conversation. Everyone talks to their animals. It's perfectly normal. Don't try to make something out of it." Keeping the book in my left hand, I head back to our food. "Now, let's clean up our dinner. I have to actually get some sleep before the looky-loos arrive tomorrow."

"Looky-loos?"

"Not sure if you're familiar, but once a month my grandmother used to open up the Rare Books Loft for research. Who knows how legitimate any of it is, but Twiggy takes all the reservations and sets up the books. Usually it's on a weekend but, as you know, she has other duties right now. So, tomorrow is the access day."

"Mind if I take a look around the loft?"

My tummy tingles and I'm almost sure my heart experiences a mild infarction. I don't trust myself enough to let him get that close to my apartment and still find the strength to bar him from accessing —the, um, apartment. "Twiggy's pretty militant about who goes into that loft. But I'm sure if you come in tomorrow morning she'll chaperone you around." I attempt to finish with a nonchalant laugh, but the tightness in my throat seems to echo off the walls of the small back room and reveal my not-so-secret discomfort.

He shrugs and walks toward the glowing red exit sign above the alley door.

Even without using my special powers, I'm easily able to pick up on Erick's disappointment. But it's better for both of us if I play dumb.

He pauses with his hand on the handle, turns back, and points to the book I'm holding. "You'll let me know if there's anything in there about that finial, right?"

"Of course. You know I'm always willing to share my intel."

"Right. I also remember that the timeline on that information disbursement is generally a little fuzzy." His broad shoulders shake with laughter as he steps into the twilight-blue alleyway.

The memory of those jeans will serve me well in dreamland this evening.

CHAPTER 8

THE WEIGHT OF A LARGE, hungry caracal sitting
on my chest forces me awake. I reach for my phone
and am pleased to discover that Mr. Cuddlekins actually allowed me to sleep in until the glorious hour
of 9:00 a.m.

Dropping the phone onto the summer-weight
down comforter, I roll over, hoping to grab another
hour's sleep.

THWACK!

Pyewacket's first strike to the back of my head is
sans claws. But history has taught me that his
second strike will be more deadly.

I scratch between his tufted ears and push him
off my chest, lovingly stroking the scar behind his
scapula from that time he took a bullet for my dad

and me. The least I can do is get up and pour him some Fruity Puffs.

Stumbling into the bathroom, I splash cool water on my face. One look in the mirror confirms: I desperately need coffee.

Hastily changing into street clothes, I throw on a weather-inappropriate knit beanie to cover my messy white haystack of a hairdo. At the last minute, I remember the throng of people that will currently be inhabiting the Rare Books Loft and add a pair of sunglasses to my ensemble.

I hit the plaster medallion and march out of my apartment with my hands shoved in the pockets of my hoodie.

Pyewacket struts out behind me, reows a warning to the intruders, and bounds down the stairs like a streak of tan lightning.

A few heads lift from their tomes, but most ignore the unwelcome intrusion.

Keeping my head down, I avoid all eye contact and rush down the stairs. The rims of the sunglasses somehow interfere with my depth perception, and I fail to raise my front foot high enough to clear the chain. The toe of my tennis shoe catches, I flail my arms in a fruitless attempt to grasp the banister, and manage to shoulder roll onto the thick carpet, just as a satisfied cackle breaks loose behind me.

"Never gets old," Twiggy manages to say between her guffaws. "Where are you headed, 8 Mile?"

From my subservient position on the floor, I manage the only reply I can think of. "8 *Mile?* Are you some kind of closet Eminem fan?"

Without missing a beat, Twiggy busts out the entire hook from Eminem's "Lose Yourself."

Awkwardly rising to my feet, I reward her with a classic slow-clap. "Now I can say I've heard everything."

"You ain't heard nothin', doll." She steps closer and whispers, "But you'd better get out of here before Ursulina sees you." Twiggy nods her head up toward the loft.

Matching her subversive tone I ask, "She's here?"

Twiggy nods.

My magicked mood ring tingles and the hairs on the back of my neck stand on end. "What book is she looking at?"

My volunteer employee pauses, looks up and to the right. "She asked to see *L'innamoramento de Orlando.*"

I shrug. "And that is . . .?"

"Some old story about a famous paladin that served Charlemagne in battle."

Pyewacket figure-eights through my legs with immense superiority. "Huh? Pye knocked a book about historical weapons off the shelf last night."

Twiggy reaches down and scratches Pyewacket's arched back. "Always said he's smarter than most humans."

I gesture toward the loft. "She doesn't know I'm the girl working the pickle stand, does she?"

Twiggy shakes her head. "Nah. She's about as observant as a wildebeest and twice as suggestible. She did ask me if I could check with my friend at the sheriff's station to see when she could pick up Edmund's things, though."

"What? Why would she be anxious to get her hands on a suit of armor?"

Twiggy shrugs. "No idea, kid."

"Will you pour Pye some Fruity Puffs? I need to get some breakfast and see if I can beg a favor from Silas."

"No problem." She walks toward the back room, and Pyewacket follows her as though he was an integral part of our entire conversation.

On my way to the diner, I call Silas. "Good morning, Mr. Willoughby. I have a favor to ask."

Silas is openly pleased with my display of manners, but is unable to meet me at the diner.

I stop in the middle of the sidewalk and shift my weight back and forth. "Well, I can't hang out in the bookshop. Today's 'research day' in the loft and some lady from the Renaissance Faire is in there. She might recognize me and blow my cover before I get the info I need."

He kindly offers to make me breakfast, if I'd like to drive out to his house. The idea catches me completely off guard. I'm ashamed to say it never occurred to me that Silas lives in a house. I suppose I always pictured him in some dusty office: dark shelves lining the walls, stuffed with huge legal tomes and smelling of pipe tobacco. I'm not sure where I imagined him spending the rest of his life, I honestly didn't think about it. The opportunity to see his house is kind of an offer I can't refuse. "Sure, text me the address."

After enduring a brief admonishment regarding the impersonal realm of texting and its destruction of the very etiquette of humanity, he gives me the address verbally and instructs me to use every facet of my mind. Which is his way of saying, "use it or lose it."

"Copy that. I'll see you soon."

I make an about-face, walk back toward the bookshop, and plan to hop in my Jeep. As I near the garages in the alley, an odd thought pops into my head. The snow has melted and the weather is officially embracing spring—just in time for summer. It's the perfect day to break out the Mercedes. I type in the code on the keypad and smile broadly as the garage door trundles up.

The view does not disappoint.

A 1957 silver Mercedes 300SL coupe with sexy, gullwing doors and an engine that begs to chew up the pavement. I whistle softly under my breath and run my hand respectfully along its curves.

Slipping into my beautiful automobile, I take my time driving along the lakeshore to see my mentor.

The bright spring sunshine glitters off the rough water like sequins on a country Western singer's costume, and white spray jets into the air as huge waves smash against the rocks. It's so hard to believe this is an enormous freshwater lake and not an inland ocean.

The narrow private road leading to Silas's home winds through a beautiful birch forest; trees wrapped in black-and-white bark as far as the eye can see. I'm sure there must be a few other varieties tucked amongst the monochromatic trunks, but the mesmerizing flickering of their beauty takes center stage.

As the dwelling in the forest looms into view, its perfect eccentricity enchants me. An awe-inspiring Gothic structure with three haunting stories and small dormers in the roof, indicating a possibly usable attic space. Sharply pointed turrets accent the corners and intricate stained-glass windows catch the morning sun. The home is not in disrepair, but it has clearly waged a lengthy battle with time and has given up a little ground with each passing year. A grey stone wall, higher than my head, encloses the property, and a black iron gate, bearing a sigil I faintly recognize, aligns with the once-grand front entrance of the home.

Parking the Mercedes, I hop out and try the gate. Despite no visible locking mechanism, the iron bars do not budge.

I call for assistance. "Hello. Yes, I'm here. The gate's locked. Yes, but— Fine. I understand. I'll see you when I see you." Apparently my lesson starts before breakfast.

Shoving my phone in my back pocket, I place a hand over the squiggly mark in the center of the gate. Silas instructed me to make use of the skill he taught me for getting out of handcuffs. He swears there's an overlap between the alchemical process of unlocking handcuffs and the method I must employ to unlock his gate.

My first two attempts end in failure and frustration.

Before making my third attempt, I close my eyes and take three deep, measured breaths. Releasing each one slowly and purposefully. I place both hands over the symbol and visualize an ice cube transitioning from its frozen state to its liquid state.

The soft scraping of a well-oiled mechanism rewards my efforts. As the final thunk of metal sounds, the gate pushes open effortlessly. I walk through shaking my head, but on high alert for additional obstacles that I may have to overcome before entering this enigmatic structure.

A frightened jump and a muffled scream escape when the gates clang shut behind me, of their own volition.

Swallowing with difficulty, I test my weight on each of the five steps as I climb toward the porch.

Reaching the door without further incident, I search the carved wooden door jams for a bell.

No joy.

I shouldn't be surprised. I'm sure Silas considers doorbells to be a scourge on polite society. I reach up and grasp the patinaed brass knocker. A graceful mermaid stretches downward and the pivot point is a brass pin through her tail. I knock her elbows twice against the brass plate beneath and wait.

As I'm reaching up to knock a third time, the handle scrapes and the massive door creaks inward.

"Good morning, Mizithra. Do come in."

And I do.

The marble floor of the foyer is polished to a

sheen and a crystal chandelier sparkles with sun-light kisses filtering through the high windows.

"Wow! You never told me you lived in a fairy-tale castle."

"One doesn't think of one's home in those terms. I simply enjoy the isolation this location pro-vides." He shuffles across the vestibule in his house slippers and turns to motion for me to follow. "We'll take breakfast in the sun room."

I stifle a chuckle and follow.

The "sun room" is a greenhouse larger than my entire rundown studio apartment back in Ari-zona. Flowering plants, citrus trees, and fresh veg-etables bring life to the space, but the heart-stopping highlight is . . . the view beyond the greenery.

The mansion sits atop a bluff overlooking the great lake, iced with whitecaps, and for a moment it's as though I've stepped through a portal to the shores of Wales or Scotland.

"Please join me, Mitzy."

The sound of his voice surprises me. I forgot I wasn't alone. The table is laid with fried eggs, sausages, scones, marmalade, clotted cream, tea, cof-fee, and orange juice. I can't hide my shock. "Do you eat like this every day?"

"I spent my youth scrimping and saving, my midlife battling for glory in the courtroom, and I plan to spend my golden years exploring the joys I overlooked."

Seems like that's his way of saying yes. "Did you make all of this today?"

He smiles and smooths his bushy grey mustache. "I have a cook who visits once a week and lays up my seven days' sustenance. I made the eggs and sausage on this day, but the remainder of the credit is undeserved."

Taking a seat, I lift the coffee carafe. "May I pour you a cup of joe?"

He nods congenially and offers his cup. "When you've finished your meal, you may enlighten me as to the true purpose of your visit."

I'm sorry to report, despite the fading opulence of the setting and the air of historic civility, I gobble up my delicious morning meal with abandon. So, I'm pretty much ready to tell my tale in five minutes.

"There was this weird thing that happened last night when I was hanging out with Erick."

Silas wipes his mouth with his napkin and harrumphs before he replies. "I'm not sure I'm the person you should be having this discussion with. Perhaps you should speak to your father about these matters."

Scrunching up my face in confusion, it takes a moment for me to decipher the meaning behind his response. After a gratifying snicker, I clarify my statement. "First of all, my dad is on a fundraising tour for the Restorative Justice Foundation and will be out of town for at least a week. And, B: It wasn't *that* kind of thing. It was a magical thing." Before I can correct myself, Silas wags a finger in my general direction.

"Do you mean a psychic occurrence or an alchemical working?"

I bow my head mockingly. "My mistake, sir. I absolutely meant a psychic thing. May I continue?"

Silas nods his head magnanimously.

"Erick and I were bantering, and he kind of challenged me to prove that I knew some stuff about him. So I said a couple things that I remembered, and then this weird sensation passed over me and I just knew everything. There were images, sounds, smells, messages. I mean— I just knew things."

"About any topic in particular?"

"Oh, yeah. I thought I said that, but yeah, about Erick's past. Like stuff from his childhood, but stuff he's never told me."

My alchemical mentor takes a sip of his coffee, dabs at his mustache with his napkin, and carefully lays the linen cloth in his lap. "Your gifts have always had an unpredictable edge. I have heard stories of spontaneous psychometry, but, to be quite forthright, I have never met a living soul who has offered more than hearsay and anecdotes. If what you claim is true—"

"It's true!" I put up my hand to prevent a lecture regarding my rude interruption. "I'm sorry, but I can assure you it's true. Erick was completely creeped out, and I had already shouted at Grams in front of him, made up a story about an imaginary cat to cover my flub, and then he saw me talking to the actual cat—"

"Easy now. Take a deep breath, Mizithra." Silas walks to the kitchen and returns with a gleaming butcher's knife. He lays the sharpened cutlery in front of me, and returns to his seat.

I wait silently. I feel the lesson brewing.

"An object, such as the one I've lain before you, has many purposes. In addition, it contains information unique to its two parts. The handle may contain information about the wielder, while the blade reveals its intent." He steeples his fingers and rhythmically bounces his thick chin on the tips.

Staring at the knife, I leave my hands in my lap and ask, "Do you want me to do something?"

Silas continues to nod. "Indeed. I wish you to produce two separate readings. Grasp the handle and blade in turn, and reveal for me the corresponding information."

Reaching up hesitantly, I grip the handle with my left hand. I close my eyes and try to push away the lingering concerns about my weird powers and my spontaneous reading. Instead, I focus on the messages in the wood. "This is your cook's favorite knife. She's left-handed. She has mild rheumatoid arthritis. Her only daughter lives in Oklahoma. Her husband died of a heart attack two years ago—"

"Fine. And now the blade." Silas unceremoniously interrupts my flow and demands an encore.

I open my eyes and have a brief pout. I'd hoped my information would receive some confirmation or at least some impressed gratitude. But, once again I'm reminded that fawning is not in my mentor's nature.

Turning the knife, I grip the steel blade, careful to avoid the deadly edge. This end of the knife is silent, in that I don't *hear* anything or receive any auditory messages, just images and feelings. It's all a bit gruesome, as the cook prefers to do a great deal of her own butchering, so I pull my hand back fairly quickly.

Silas leans forward and his jowls shake as he moves his head back and forth. "Nothing?"

"Nothing I want to repeat." I push the blade of the knife away with one finger "I can say for certain, your cook is a skilled butcher."

Silas chuckles and claps his gnarled hands together. "Well done. Now tell me the purpose of your visit."

You have to admire his persistence. "This morning, Twiggy mentioned that the dead man's wife was reading a book in the loft and had also asked her to call in a favor at the sheriff's station to get her husband's personal effects released."

"Which book?"

"I can't remember the title, it sounded vaguely Italian. But it was something about a paladin and Charlemagne."

"You are certain?"

"As certain as I can be, not speaking Italian and whatnot."

Silas gets to his feet with remarkable agility. "And these personal effects?"

I shrug. "He was killed in the middle of a joust. He was wearing a suit of armor and probably not much else."

He strides toward me and grips my shoulder firmly. His milky-blue eyes pierce mine. "Was there a sword?"

"Hang on." Using another of the many skills he's taught me, I close my eyes and replay the memory of that joust. With my extra senses engaged, I clearly see every piece of the Lord Mayor's garb. He indeed has a scabbard and a sword. "Yes. There was a scabbard and a sword. Which is weird, right? Do knights usually wear swords in a joust?"

"That is hardly our concern. We must find that sword before it falls into the wrong hands."

"What do you mean? If it was part of the Lord Mayor's costume, it can't possibly be a bad thing to give it back to his wife."

"In fairness, I fear I must withhold some information to prevent unduly influencing your future reading."

I shake my head and pour myself another cup of liquid alert. "If that stuff is locked up in evidence at the station, I honestly don't see how we're going to get our hands on it."

"Take a stroll through the garden, down to the water's edge, and renew your strength while I make a selection of potentially auspicious phone calls."

And Erick thinks I'm a conundrum. Silas makes the riddle of the Sphinx seem like a nursery rhyme. I clear up the dishes and set them on the grey-green soapstone counter in the kitchen. However, the beauty of the outdoors calls to me and I take Silas's suggestion.

Exiting through a side door in the sun room, I enter his immaculately landscaped backyard. There are four separate gardens, each with meticulously cared for plants, and every bit of greenery is carefully labeled with brass plaques on sturdy posts.

On the left, the first garden consists of herbs that I mostly recognize by sight, even if the displayed Latin names don't ring a bell. Sage, chamomile, thyme, oregano, and many more. My brief employment at the plant nursery definitely gives me a leg up in this quadrant. To my right are flowers and small flowering shrubs. As I proceed across the slate terrace and down two steps, the lower garden plot unfolds on the left, containing a multitude of plants most would consider poisonous, including wolfsbane. A chill creeps over my skin, and I hurry through the lowest level of the patio and across the lawn toward a knee-high granite wall.

When I reach the edge of the safe and inviting lawn, I gasp at the magnificent rocky cliffs revealing a sheer drop into the wild waters below.

Stepping back from the awe-inspiring view, I close my eyes and let the sun share its warmth while the wind howls up the cliff face, threatening to topple me backward.

I know Silas hates it when I mistakenly label alchemical workings as magical, but there is magic in this place. I can feel it swirling up from the earth and filling me up. After making fun of energy, vortexes, and spiritual readings for so many years when I lived in Sedona, the irony of me embracing the magic of nature on a windswept break above a powerful and enormous body of water is not lost on me.

"Mitzy, we have an appointment at the sheriff's station. Shall we take my car or yours?"

The trance is broken and I wander away from the majestic view with mild regret. "Mine, Silas, always mine." I've only had a couple of rides in his 1908 Model T and I intend to cap that number. Wait, did he say we have an appointment with the sheriff?

CHAPTER 9

As we wind our way toward the town of Pin Cherry Harbor, Silas impresses me with his quick thinking. While I enjoyed the simple beauty of the wild morning, he and Twiggy cooked up quite a scheme.

"My first telephone call was to the bookshop. Twiggy and I discussed, at length, Ursulina and the tome she was perusing, as well as the possibility that she may require legal representation."

Nodding my head, I smile. "Nice."

Silas smooths his mustache with a thumb and forefinger. "Perhaps it will be perceived as kind, but the gesture was quite self-serving, I assure you."

I roll my eyes. Of course, Silas completely missed the sarcasm in my compliment. "Copy that. Please continue."

"Shortly after discussing this rudimentary plan with Twiggy, I received a phone call from Mrs. Ursulina."

"Don't you mean, Mrs. Gurney?"

"I do not. While Ursulina was indeed married to Edmund Gurney, she did not share his last name. In fact, the singular morpheme 'Ursulina' appears to be her full, legal name, according to the details of our brief exchange."

Taking one hand off the steering wheel, I adjust my beanie and exhale. "Interesting. Like Madonna or Cher."

Silas wags his head and his jowls wiggle. "Not exactly, my dear. There is a difference between a singular full, legal name and an alias. In the case of Madonna, for instance, her actual name is Madonna Louise Ciccone—"

Eager to end the lecture, I interrupt. "Got it. Please continue with the rest of your plan. I get the name thing."

"Yes. I offered my services to Ursulina pro bono, as I am an ardent supporter of the Renaissance Faire."

"She bought that?"

Silas tilts his head and brushes a bit of lint from the lapel of his tweed coat. "I beg your pardon?"

"I mean, you're not actually a Rennie, are you?"

"I shall not bandy about tales of old, but suffice

to say I am a generous financial supporter of the arts."

"Good to know."

Silas tugs at his seatbelt to gain access to one of his pockets and produces a butterscotch candy. The never-ending crinkling of the cellophane wrapper sends me into a fit of giggles.

"What amuses you, my dear?"

"It's nothing. Sorry, please finish your story."

"After a pleasant exchange of formalities and a verbal agreement of representation, I assured Ursulina that I would retrieve her husband's personal effects and deliver them to her caravan—"

"Wait? What? So after all that, we don't even get to snoop around?"

Silas chuckles until his cheeks redden, his shoulders shake, and an amused tear leaks from the corner of his left eye.

Before he has a chance to answer, I recognize the flaw in my logic. "I figured it out." After a brief silence, I ask a follow-up question. "Should I drive back to the bookshop and swap this out for the Jeep? I'm not exactly sure a suit of armor will fit inside this thing."

Silas pats his chest and breathes deeply to recover from his amusement. "That would be prudent. And if you had allowed me to complete my thought, I told Ursulina that it would take a few days to process the request and I would deliver Mr. Gurney's personal effects by the end of the week."

"Oh. I got a little overexcited. That should be plenty of time."

"For snooping?" Silas snickers.

I lift my chin and exhale haughtily. "For proper investigating."

After swapping the vehicles and driving to the station, Silas advises me to wait in the Jeep while he completes the necessary paperwork and retrieves the physical items.

As much as I would enjoy a little banter with Furious Monkeys, the deputy who mans the front desk and endlessly plays said game on her phone, and perhaps a peek at Sheriff Too-Hot-To-Handle, I have to agree with Silas. If he shows up alone, his legal counsel cover story should hold water. If we show up together, our collusion will be blatantly obvious.

He shuffles into the station and I turn on the radio to entertain myself while I wait.

As luck would have it, I barely catch the last fifteen seconds of one song before it's time for the Birch County local news. The deep, masculine voice of the radio announcer indicates that Grant Schweiger could face first-degree murder charges in association with the recent death of Edmund Gurney, also known as the Lord Mayor of the Renaissance Faire. As his voice drones on with additional details about the Faire's continued operation, local bingo night info, and weather, my mind drifts back to that first day at the arena.

I play the scene through from beginning to end as I search the periphery for any clues I might have missed, attempting to push my extrasensory perceptions to their limits. The Royal box is full, the knights' squires look dutiful but uninterested, the hype men and women selling flags in each sector are fully occupied with their tasks, and Grant approaches the final charge with the persistent exactitude of the previous two.

And then everything blurs.

As I mentally fast-forward, past Grant's capture, to my investigation of the arena, I freeze-frame the vision at the moment I popped that piece of sugar glass in my mouth.

"The sugar glass!" The back hatch of the Jeep squeaks open and the fright causes my chest to constrict violently. I've gotten so used to Ghost-ma popping in and out of rooms at the bookshop and museum, I had almost forgotten this visceral level of fear. My head whips around as Silas juggles an enormous parcel in one hand, and a stack of papers in the other.

Hustling out of the Jeep, I run to the back and

help him maneuver the armor and sword into the back.

"Thank you, Mitzy."

Back inside the vehicle, I asked the obvious question. "Now what? We can't take this haul to the bookshop, and I definitely need some privacy to see if I can read anything from the items."

Silas opens his mouth to answer, but before he can utter a sound, I blurt, "I forgot about the sugar glass!"

He shakes his head with disappointment. "I had hoped I wouldn't live to see the obliteration of manners, but I fear that day has come."

"Honestly, again, I'm sorry. It's just that I've already forgotten it once, and I didn't want to forget again." My weak smile pleads for mercy, and I continue, "The spike on the end of the lance was covered with a dome of sugar glass. That stuff is not easy to make, I can assure you. For someone to make such an intricate casing, they'd have to have experience. It was strong enough to withstand bumping and jostling, but just the right thickness to crack and reveal the spike on direct impact. We need to look into that."

Silas nods slowly. "Perhaps we may return to my domicile with Edmund Gurney's personal effects. Once you complete your inspection, I shall contact my client and schedule a delivery."

"Right, I keep forgetting you have a house."

Silas harrumphs and grips the "oh no" handle above the passenger-side window as I make a screeching U-turn on Main Street and eventually head east on Shoreline Drive, back to the Gothic castle in the enchanted wood.

As we rumble down the private drive, Silas gestures for me to take a right onto a previously hidden side road. I didn't notice it on my first pass. Maybe I was too mesmerized by the trees.

The secret route takes us to the rear of the house and a three-car garage.

"The stall closest to the house is empty. I'll open the garage door and you can pull in."

I stop on the flagstone and Silas exits the Jeep.

Once inside the garage, he directs me to bring Edmund's things to a sturdy table in the "keeping room."

"What the heck is a 'keeping room' and why do you have one?"

He answers as he leads the way. "A keeping or hearth room is a traditional space in a Victorian Gothic. It is generally nearest to the kitchen or larder and is the warmest room in the home." He sighs. "To be fair, the library has a larger table, but it is all the way on the other side of the house, and time is of the essence." He gestures to the thick oak sideboard, scarred with age. "Place the items here."

"Copy that." I lay the pieces of the suit of armor out on the table, as though they are the bones of a body on any one of a hundred criminal investigative shows I've watched over the years. I place the sword, the *pièce de résistance*, on top of the "knight." Stepping back, I smile proudly. "There. Perfect."

Silas lowers himself into one of the cozy chairs nestled near the massive stone fireplace. "In the interest of time, I'll ask you to focus your reading on the sword alone. Please remove it from the scabbard and grip the hilt with both hands."

I carefully do as I'm told, and as soon as my hands grip the weapon, information washes over me in a deluge.

My heart races and everything is swirling together in a confusing mélange. I can't catch my breath.

A commanding voice cuts through the noise. "Kneel. Place the sword on the floor and touch it with the index finger of your left hand."

I'm not sure if I'm choosing to follow the instructions or if I'm compelled, but the next thing I know I'm on my knees with one finger on the intricately embellished hilt.

"Take a deep breath. Clear your head and request the sword's provenance."

Once again, the actions seem to have a mind of

their own. This time there is a deep calm, as though I'm occupying the moment before the sword came to be, and then a light washes over me so bright and pure that it brings tears to my eyes.

"An angel," I whisper.

"Yes," replies Silas, in steadfast agreement. "Accept his gift and push on."

I take the sword and time swirls past me in chunks.

"A challenge . . . A fair maiden . . . I'm a soldier. No, more than that—a paladin . . . I serve a great leader."

I shiver as images of far too many battles rush through my mind. All at once, I feel the killing blow. The final moment. Panic fills my heart and I know I must hide the sword from the advancing army.

"This divine sword must not fall into the wrong hands."

"And it will not," Silas serenely replies.

I hide the sword beneath my horse's body and darkness swallows all.

"It's over, the images—"

"Patience."

No sooner does Silas speak, than a ray of light touches the steel.

"A farmer."

A series of poor families through the ages hand

the sword down from father to son, until its origin is utterly lost. The messages and images fast forward to the present day, and I see and hear a modern flea market. I recognize Ursulina, minus her Rennie finery, and I assume the man standing next to her is the Lord Mayor. I never saw Edmund's face. His helmet somehow stayed on, even when he was unhorsed.

"Edmund bought it at a flea market. I don't believe he had any idea what he was buying." Opening my eyes, I take my finger off the sword. "Did I actually see an angel?"

Silas smooths his mustache with a thumb and forefinger. "I believe your vision recreated the moment this sword was gifted to a mortal. It is my hypothesis that this sword is—"

"Durendal!" I shout the name and grip my chest in shock. "I don't know where that came from."

"Indeed. Durendal was given to Roland, the paladin of Charlemagne by an archangel. Popular legend concludes that Roland cast the sword over a cliff to prevent it falling into enemy hands, but I have always believed the sword lived on—waiting for a return to glory." He thoughtfully tamps his mustache. "I fear it is no coincidence that Ursulina chose to peruse *L'innamoramento de Orlando*."

"Why?"

"The title translates to Orlando, or Roland, in love. The poem concerns the heroic knight who was that sword's first mortal master."

Staring at the holy relic with a new appreciation, I'm thankful I didn't have to touch the blade. With a memory of the cook's favorite knife still fresh in my mind, I'm happy to skip the cut-reel for a paladin's sword. "Ursulina said in her statement to the sheriff that Edmund liked to collect old junk. And from the information in the vision, he had no idea what he was buying at that flea market."

Silas exhales slowly. "Someone did."

CHAPTER 10

AFTER A QUICK LAYING of hands on the armor, Silas calls it. The reading is over. He takes a thick linen cloth from a drawer in a small end table in the keeping room and wraps it around the hilt. He holds the sword as though it is a rattlesnake and carefully navigates through his house.

I follow several steps behind, and when we arrive in his library I nod appreciatively. Now, this is where I pictured Silas. He steps toward a life-sized marble statue of Hermes Trismegistus, according to the placard, and presses on the great toe of his left foot.

A section of the bookcase glides open, across the marble floor, and a vault door is revealed.

"Impressive," I mumble. "I'm guessing you gave

Isadora a hand in creating the secret doors and compartments at my bookshop."

He ignores my commentary and holds his hand over the locking mechanism of the vault. He mumbles a lengthy bit of Latin and the wheel spins under its own power. He pulls open the door and places the legendary blade inside.

"What else do you have in there?" I step forward, but a strange thickness in the air prevents me from walking past the statue.

Silas closes the vault, mutters a great deal of Latin and possibly some German, and steps back as the bookcase swings home to conceal the hidden mysteries.

As soon as the cabinet clicks into place the thickness in the air vanishes and I stumble forward. "That's a fascinating security system."

"And effective," he says with a matter-of-fact nod of his jowls. "Will you be joining me for a midday meal?"

While I'm eager to see what other delectable treasures his cook has "laid up," my conscience gets the best of me. "Shouldn't we tell Erick what we know about the sword?"

"Perhaps."

"It just seems important, Silas. If a valuable item like that is involved, it definitely moves suspicion away from Grant and back toward Ursulina."

"Whom I now represent."

"Oops." I lift my hands helplessly. "Three steps forward and two steps back?"

"It would behoove me not to fracture the protections of attorney/client privilege. However, if you wish to enjoy a casual lunch with your special friend, far be it from me to intervene." Silas walks behind a massive desk and takes a seat in an enormous leather chair that resembles a throne.

The fact that he called Erick a special friend gives me a secret fit of giggles, since I'm always accusing Grams of having an undisclosed number of special friends in her lifetime. "Are you sure there's not some loophole that would allow you to join me?"

"I am sorry, Mizithra, but I must uphold a certain set of standards. And I would be doing my client a grave injustice if I were to cast her to the wolves simply on a whim."

"Whim? You think that vision I had was a whim?"

Silas harrumphs. "Absolutely not. However, knowledge of the sword's provenance is hardly knowledge of the murderer. I suggest you discuss your findings with the sheriff and search for other avenues toward the obscured truth."

As I turn to leave, a sudden thought occurs. "Would it be all right if I say that you have a bunch of knowledge about old weapons? I need some explanation other than visions of angels. It may have worked for Hildegard of Bingen and Joan of Arc, but Mitzy Moon would prefer to keep that on the DL."

He steeples his fingers and slowly bounces his chin on the tips. "I am not certain as to what 'DL' refers, but I find that honesty is the best policy."

"But—"

Silas holds up a finger, which clearly instructs me to wait for additional information. "And the truth is, I happen to possess a great deal of knowledge in the field of ancient weaponry and armor."

I exhale and bow to the master. "I never doubted you for a minute, Silas."

His chuckle echoes down the grand hall as I thread my way through his veritable mansion back to the Jeep.

Reversing out of the garage, I start typing a text to Erick, but stop. I jump out of the vehicle, pull the garage door closed, and call the station. As soon as the call is transferred to him, I hear the strain in his voice and hope I can ease it. "Hey, I know you're swamped right now, but I have some potentially great news, and I kinda need to give it to you face-to-face. Trust me, it's worth it. Can you meet me for lunch at the diner?"

He makes a couple of excuses, which honestly

sound quite valid, but I quickly play my trump card. "The intel might clear Grant."

Not surprisingly, Erick agrees to meet me in twenty minutes.

As I drive back into town, I go over the details of my story. I can use a lot of the information from my vision, and simply attribute it to Silas. However, I can't wait to get back to the bookshop and tell Grams the real story—that I saw an angel.

Myrtle's Diner is roughly half full. There are a number of locals whom I recognize and some vaguely familiar faces that I hope aren't Rennies. I tug my beanie down and tuck away any loose strands of my white hair.

Odell's quizzical face peeks through the orders-up window and he raises an eyebrow.

I shake my head, shrug, and slip into the corner booth with one eye on the door, anxiously awaiting Erick's arrival.

The easy-on-the-eyes lawman arrives a few minutes later. He salutes Odell and slips onto the bench seat across from mine. His polyester uniform pants squeak lightly against the vinyl.

I walk my fingers across the table and turn my hand palm up, in what I hope is an obvious invitation. "Thanks for making time for me."

Erick's sexy smile turns my insides all melty,

and when he lays his strong hand in mine a thrill rushes over my skin.

"So what's this big break in the case, Moon?"

When we first met, he would use my last name as a way of keeping things "all business," but now I find it endearing. Especially when he squeezes my hand playfully as he says it. I rub my thumb along his pinky as I reply, "I'm not sure if you're aware, but Silas is kind of like an ancient weapons expert." I widen my eyes innocently and wait for his response.

"Here it comes." He withdraws his strong hand and eyes me accusingly. "I knew there was an ulterior motive behind Silas representing Ursulina. This is starting to sound like a conflict of interest."

"Technically, you can tack it up to hearsay, since Silas refuses to have any part in sharing this information with you." I wink and wait for permission.

"Fine, strictly off the record. What've you got?"

"The sword that the Lord Mayor was wearing at the time of his death is worth a fortune. It's not a piece of flea-market junk; it's actually the sword that belonged to Roland the Paladin of Charlemagne. It was rumored to be the sharpest sword in history and it was given to Roland by an archangel."

Erick leans back and rubs the stubble on his

chin thoughtfully. "I wish I could say that changes things."

"How does it not? Whoever killed the Lord Mayor had to know about the sword. That clearly points the finger at Ursulina."

"Not exactly. The problem is the Lord Mayor was a hoarder; he never got rid of anything. Even though the Faire was in some financial trouble, he wouldn't sell off a single piece in his collection. Maybe Ursulina was trying to set up a side deal, or maybe Grant saw an opportunity to make some extra cash and quit the knight business."

"I don't think he wanted out. The squire I talked to made it sound like Grant was a hero in the Ren Faire knight community. He perfected the unhorsing stunt and made his mark. Do you think he needed the money? Did he have another gig in the off-season? You looked into his finances, right?"

He chuckles at my rapid-fire questions. "We subpoenaed the records. We're waiting for them to come through."

"What about Simon? If he's partners with the Lord Mayor and Ursulina, he has a motive. I mean, he *made* the spike. And if the Faire is in as much financial trouble as you say, he might've wanted to get his hands on that sword to save his investment. He's a good blacksmith. He must know something about weapons. Wouldn't he have recognized the metalwork?"

He nods thoughtfully. "If that sword truly is Durendal—"

"How do you know the name of Roland's sword?"

Erick blushes adorably and looks down at the table. "I was a lonely kid with a lot of time on my hands, okay?"

I shrug and grin wistfully. "Hey, no judgment. I was raised by television families after my mom passed."

He smiles tenderly. "I'm sorry I never got to meet your mom."

My throat tightens and my emotional shields go up. "Me too," is all I can manage.

Noticing my discomfort, he kindly changes the subject. "Anyway, the legend I read was that Roland threw the sword over a cliff and it's still there to this day. It's a little bit rusty and it's been chained in place to prevent theft. So, unless Simon had insider knowledge, he'd have no reason to suspect that the sword in the Lord Mayor's scabbard was Durendal."

Before I can stop myself I blurt, "But Roland didn't throw the sword off a cliff. He hid the sword under his horse's body to protect it from the enemy and then some farmers found it and they passed it down generation to generation—" My eyes widened, I swallow loudly, and lean back in my seat.

Odell sets our meals on the table, glances from me to Erick, and quietly slips away.

Erick places a thin paper napkin in his lap and his reply is laced with suspicion. "I'm starting to wonder if Silas is actually a weapons expert or if there's a bit more to this story?"

"Boy, this food sure looks good." As I dig into my burger and fries, there's a snicker from the other side of the table.

Erick busies himself with his taco salad and an odd silence hangs between us.

"Did I mention I have to go out and work at the Faire today?" I pick up my last french fry and savor it.

Erick scrunches up his face and takes a drink of his tea before he replies. "But the Faire is only open on weekends."

"That's what I thought too. But apparently Lady Natalia called Queen Twiggy this morning and told her that they want to put a second pickle cart into service next weekend, for Festival Friday, and she knew I was eager for extra work."

Erick covers his mouth with the back of his hand and chuckles mercilessly.

"Rude."

"Hey, it's your undercover gig. I'm just pleased to see how it's paying off for you." He continues to enjoy intermittent chuckles at my expense while he finishes his taco salad.

I sit opposite him in the booth, having a good old-fashioned pout.

"So when do you need to leave?" he asks.

"I was planning on heading out there right after lunch. Do you think people wear their costumes during the week? When they're working on stuff?"

He shrugs. "I kind of doubt it. I gotta say, I'm actually a little intrigued. I'll expect a full report."

I lean forward, tilt my head, and ask, "And when, exactly, will I be giving this report?"

He stretches his left hand across the table and glides his finger down my arm. "There's something I'd like to show you out on Fish Hawk Island."

I take a moment to enjoy the delectable tingles as his finger creates goosebumps on my flesh. "Wait, Fish Hawk Island is the one with the fancy restaurant, right? And then, Hawk Island is the one with the casino that I don't ever want to return to. Have I got that straight?"

He grins, as I'm sure he recalls my one and only trip to the Hawk Island Casino. "You're mostly right. Fish Hawk Island is where Nimkii runs Chez Osprey. However, I happen to know that there's something far more interesting out there, and tomorrow is my day off. How do you feel about a day trip?"

I'm only able to take shallow breaths as I imagine spending an entire day alone with him. I have to dig the fingernails of one hand into my palm to keep from blurting out my true feelings of unfettered excitement and anticipation while I search for a casual response. "Sounds divine." My cheeks flush. What is it with me and that word? I hurry to distract him from my nonsense. "I wouldn't mind grabbing dinner at Chez Osprey though."

"Deal. Dress for adventure and pack a change of clothes."

"Oh boy—"

Erick sits back, crosses his muscular arms over his chest and chews on his bottom lip for a second. "Let me guess, your *grandmother* is going to be very excited about picking out your outfits?"

The shrill staccato of my forced laughter echoes off the black-and-white linoleum. It's not like I run around claiming to be a great actress. At least not when the character I'm playing is *myself.* I slide out of the booth before I can utter any sort of incriminating response and nod my thanks to Odell.

Mumbling a hasty goodbye to Erick, I beat it back to the bookshop.

When I present Grams with my weekday Ren Faire wardrobe conundrum, she does not disappoint. "So, if you're running with the idea that your naturally white hair is actually a wig when you're in costume on the weekends, then you probably better choose a wig and pretend that is your regular hair today. And you can, of course, wear sunglasses. It's June. Nothing suspicious about that at all."

She swirls around and rockets through the wall into my *Sex and the City* meets *Confessions of a Shopaholic* closet. I join her and open the large built-in drawer at the bottom of an impressive stack, which contains a collection of wigs and hairpieces. We select a shoulder-length, mousy-brown number with bangs.

"You'll blend right in. There's some Gucci sunglasses in that top drawer on the left."

"Gucci?" I shake my head. "I better stop and pick up a cheap pair from the Piggly Wiggly. I'm supposed to be a poor college student desperate for summer work, remember?"

Grams claps her translucent hands together and giggles. "I just love a good backstory."

My expanding wig expertise allows me to slip the faux hair into place with ease and, of course, the requisite smattering of bobby pins.

Grams is eager to hear my report when I return. As the bookcase door slides closed behind me, I toss her a tantalizing treat. "Oh, I almost forgot. Erick and I are going out to Fish Hawk Island tomorrow for a day trip, and he said to bring a change of clothes for Chez Osprey."

Her ghostly squeal echoes through the bookshop as I race down the wrought-iron circular staircase to my Jeep.

CHAPTER 11

ARRIVING AT THE BACK GATE of the Renaissance Faire on a not-open-for-business day is a bit like stepping behind the curtain in the *Wizard of Oz*. The faces look somewhat familiar, but without their elaborate garb and phony accents, the magic evaporates. I push my dime-store sunglasses into place and head to the existing pickle stand, hoping that Joan will be on-site to give me instructions and assistance regarding pickle palace part deux.

As I approach the pickle stand, I observe Joanie and Simon in a heated argument. The two of them normally seem so close that it's hard for me to imagine what they could possibly be fighting about. I stop and pretend to tie my shoelace.

"Why did you get involved with her, Simon? I told you she was poison."

"For the twentieth time, Joanie, I wasn't involved with her. She's lying. I don't know why, but she's absolutely lying. I promise."

Peeking over the top of my sunglasses, I see Joan cross her arms and turn away from her half-brother.

He places a strong hand on her shoulder. "Joanie, please. You're not just my sister, you're my best friend. I can't stand it when you're mad at me."

Her arms slowly unwrap and fall to her sides. "Promise? I see the way she looks at you. I know it's, like, definitely crossed her mind."

"She looks at everybody like that. It's probably just to get back at the Lord Mayor. I'm not even sure she would follow through."

Joanie flicks his hand off her shoulder and places a hand on either hip. "Are you defending her now?"

"I'm not defending anyone, except myself. I didn't have an affair with Ursulina. That's the truth. If I can't even get my own sister to believe me, how do you think the cops are gonna react?"

"Maybe you should've thought of that before you made her that deadly spike."

Simon hangs his head, and I have to push my psychic senses into the mix to hear his mumbled regret.

"I feel terrible about it, Joanie. Just terrible, okay?"

She's quick to put a hand on his shoulder and pat his back. "Sorry. It's not your fault. And I do believe you."

I finish fake tying my shoe and jog to the pickle stand.

Joanie eyes me with irritation when I stop next to the cart. "Does it look like we're open?"

The tone catches me off guard. "It's me, Arwen. I know, I look different without the wig and the elf ears."

She presses a hand to her chest." Oh, my gosh, I'm so sorry. I was such a 'B' right then. I just thought you were some mundane that snuck in the back and thought they were going to get a pickle on Tuesday!"

We share a laugh, but Simon doesn't join in.

His deep voice shatters the humor. "What's your real name?"

Clearly there is no convincing him that it's Arwen. So I dig into my rather shallow bag of tricks and pull out my previous Birch County Community College fake identity and reply. "Darcy Brown."

His clenched jaw softens momentarily and Joanie giggles. "Can I just call you Arwen? Like, after this Ren Faire ends we'll probably never see each other again, and I kinda already have you pegged as an Arwen in my brain. Plus, I never imagined you had brown hair! Your white wig is so realistic."

If she only knew. I smile awkwardly. "Oh, thanks. Yeah, you can totally call me Arwen."

Simon growls a little under his breath, and my extra senses pick up on serious suspicion.

I better get straight to work and not push my luck with an interrogation, just yet. "So Lady Natalia asked me to come in and help set up another pickle stand. Do you know anything about that?"

Joanie rolls her eyes violently. "Everyone is talking about how this three-day weekend is going to be the highest attendance in history. I suppose it could be true, but how many pickles do people need? Plus, if we open the other stand, you and I can't work together, and it'll just be me over here by myself and you over there by yourself, and I don't see how that's gonna give anyone any additional pickle access." She crosses her arms and huffs, and I'm unable to stop myself from laughing.

"What?"

Struggling to catch my breath, I reply, "I don't know. Something about debating the finer points of pickle access—it just got me, you know?"

Now Joanie laughs uncontrollably and smacks her chest with an open hand as she squeals.

A quiet but not unkind voice cuts through the hilarity. "Are you gonna need any help getting that second pickle cart into position?"

"Thanks, Simon, I'm pretty sure I will. Plus, I don't exactly know where it's supposed to go."

Joan nods and waves both hands at us. "Okay, bye-bye you two. I'll work on repainting this sign, and you guys get the other stand put in place. Let me know if you need any help over there, okay?"

I flash her the thumbs up and follow Simon to the second cart.

We walk in silence, but a snoopy girl like me can only take so much. "Have you heard who's going to play the Black Knight next weekend?"

Simon shakes his head but offers no verbal response.

"So, Joanie said you made that spike, you know, *the* spike."

Simon stops abruptly and turns to face me with a steely threat in his eye.

I quickly put my hands up and shake my head. "No. No. I'm not accusing you of anything. I get that you were only doing your job. I was just wondering if you knew who puts the lances together? I mean, do the knights build their own weaponry or are their squires responsible?"

Simon does not resume his trajectory. Instead,

he widens his stance as waves of frustration and concern roll off him.

How does one move a mountain? That seems like a philosophical question that I don't have time to break down. "Look, it's my first time working at a Renaissance Faire, all right. Also, I'm stupidly curious. My nickname in college is Curious George. So, wipe that look off your face and imagine what it must be like to be me for a semester."

My self-deprecating lies have the desired effect, and Simon's demeanor shifts from impenetrable-fortress-style defensiveness to more of a draw-bridge-could-be-lowered style. He chews the inside of his cheek and stares at me.

"Also, in case I forgot to apologize, I'm so sorry I took those tongs from your forge. When Ursulina caught me wandering around, I panicked." In my mind I can hear the gears turning, as the chain un-rolls and the drawbridge descends.

He exhales and his shoulders loosen their grip on his massive neck. "Did she leave with you or hang around after she handed you my tongs?"

I pretend that I have to think long and hard be-fore I answer. "I'm pretty sure she stayed behind."

His right hand balls into a fist. "Figures. That's probably when she planted it."

"Planted what?"

The drawbridge halts and he snarls his answer.

"I'll tell you the same thing I told the cops. I made that piece for her last winter, at the forge on my private property. When the police searched the Forge of Destiny they found my design sketches for the finial. Those drawings weren't there when the sheriff took me into custody."

I'm pleased the sunglasses hide the excited gleam in my eyes. What a juicy tidbit I've uncovered. "So, you think Ursulina planted the drawings? Why?"

"That's what I can't figure out. It seems like a pretty harsh thing to do to a guy who—" He stops abruptly and his eyes dart from side to side.

"A guy who what?" I gently prompt.

His moose-sized shoulders hunch and he leans toward me. "This stays between me and you, okay? Don't go blabbing anything to Joanie."

Lifting my fingers in the salute that I've seen my father do many times, I say, "Scouts honor."

At least that brings a chuckle to Simon's lips.

I can almost hear the satisfying thud of his thick wooden drawbridge landing on the ground and welcoming me in.

"Ursulina propositioned me. She couldn't pay for the piece, because the Lord Mayor spends all their money on this Faire and on collecting trash from flea markets. She made up some story about having money hidden away, but he found it, and now the only way she could pay me was . . . Well, you know."

I'm pretty sure I do know, but I'm greedy for a little more information. "Did you accept her payment?"

Now both of Simon's hands ball into fists and the veins in his very wide, very powerful neck bulge. "No way. Why does everyone think that woman is something special? I never wanted anything to do with her. I only took the commission because I needed the money to help my parents."

Before he can close up on me, I need to give him a reason to trust me. "I believe you, Simon. I haven't been here that long, but I've seen the way Ursulina manipulates people." None of that is true, but more flies with honey.

"Thanks. Seems like you're the only one who does believe me."

Smiling warmly, I nod and put a hand on his thick arm. "Thanks for offering to help me get that pickle cart moved into position. If you happen to know anything about who assembles the lances or where they're stored, would you mind telling me?"

He turns and resumes his walk toward a large wooden storage building and surprisingly shares what he knows as we go.

According to his begrudging info, the lances are sourced from a manufacturer in the Midwest, and any squire can assemble them when they arrive. They're stored in the tack room behind the arena.

Not nearly as helpful as I'd hoped. By the time we get the pickle cart into position and I scrub the layers of dust off, from top to bottom, the sky has turned a strange shade of yellowish black. There's a crack of thunder that nearly stops my heart, and within seconds the heavens open and a deluge of warm summer rain dumps from above.

I pour the dirty water out of my bucket, wring out the rag, and run to the supply building.

The dirt beneath the straw on the pathways quickly turns to slippery mud. And my empty pail is filling up fast.

The supply shed is locked, so I hook the bucket over a post outside and hustle to the parking lot. I'm soaked to the skin by the time I arrive. My feet are making great sucking, slushy, sludgy sounds inside my shoes.

Fishing the keys out of my pocket, I dive into the oasis of dryness within the Jeep.

Off with the disgusting, muddy shoes and the wet socks.

I'd love to rip off this gross, dripping wig, but there's no point in blowing my cover when I'm so close to the truth.

I drive away from the Faire and sift through my facts. As thunder crashes and lightning crackles in the ominous storm-laden sky, I can't help but wonder how and why Ursulina orchestrated the murder of her husband. She went out of her way to set up Simon and she's clearly anxious to get her hands on that sword. But how does Grant fit into all of it?

There are too many pieces. Too many things that don't seem connected.

Home for a hot shower and some dry clothes, and then it's time for Grams and me to set up the murder wall.

CHAPTER 12

AFTER MY SHOWER, I slip into comfy summer pajamas and wheel out the large corkboard Twiggy procured for me. The first time I asked for tacks and string to create a murder wall, she refused to allow me to make holes in the lath and plaster. But necessity is the mother of invention, and now that Grams and I have gotten the hang of this, she writes the cards while I organize the board. Of course, I still have to use green yarn, because red gives her the heebie-jeebies. And who wants to scare a ghost, right?

"I appreciate you taking my feelings into consideration, Mitzy."

"There's no time for your thought-dropping or your sass, Grams. You need to focus all your energy on writing those cards. What have you got so far?"

"I have Lord Mayor, Ursulina, Grant, and Justin squire-boy."

Nodding, I tap my lips with one finger. "On the squire-boy card, write Jacob's Ladder, and then we need to make a card for Simon, and one for Joan—I guess. I don't actually suspect her of anything, but right now we're just looking for connections, and she loves gossip."

Grams salutes me. "All good investigations require a murder wall. I've seen you work magic with this thing. I'm behind it one hundred percent."

"Thanks. It's been such a weird day, and it's sort of nice to just have someone agree with me. No questions asked."

Grams giggles. "Don't count your chickens before they're hatched, young lady. If I have something to say, I'll say it."

I shake my head and pace in front of the murder wall/corkboard.

As each connection comes to mind, I run a green thread between the names.

In the end, the web of emerald lines offers no help. In a tight-knit community like the Rennies, everyone knows everyone. "All" connected is about as helpful as none.

"Ree-oow." A gentle reminder.

Pyewacket's message stops me in my tracks. "Right. The wedding ring."

Grams floats down from her lofty perch. "But that was my ring, and I'm not connected to these folks."

"Pye deals in the abstract rather than the concrete. The wedding ring is a symbol. There has to be some other connection to the married couple, Ursulina and the Lord Mayor . . . Some person or influence that we're missing."

"Well, you said the Lord Mayor was a lecherous cad, dear. Have you checked into his conquests or their husbands?"

"I did say that, but he seemed to prey on young, single women—according to Joan—so I don't think there are any angry husbands to find. I thought maybe his wife got sick of his antics and tried to manipulate someone into getting rid of him. But the lead about Ursulina having an affair with Simon was a dead end. At least if Simon was honest with me."

Grams hovers at eye level and taps one ring-ensconced finger on her lips. "Was he?"

I shrug. "I guess."

"Mizithra, you have to learn to embrace your powers. You've spoken to the man. You don't have to guess. Lean into your gifts, dear. Is he to be believed or not?"

My cheeks flush self-consciously. "Oh, right. Give me a minute." Replaying my discussion with

Simon, in full-psychic Technicolor, I pay special attention to my extra senses as he pleads his innocence.

An anxious Ghost-ma swirling around definitely distracts me from total concentration, but I do my best to shut out the otherworldly fidget spinner.

"Anything?" She's so close now I can, quite literally, feel her under my skin.

"I'm not getting any messages that indicate Simon was lying to me. I honestly think he turned her down, like he said."

Grams goes horizontal, and her noncorporeal form seems to be floating in an invisible pool of water.

"What are you doing?"

"Oh, I used to get my visions mostly when I lay down. So I was trying to force one and see if I could get any other information about Ursulina."

"Seriously? Have you been getting more after-life clairvoyant-y and not telling me?"

"No, dear. Nothing like that. It's just that spending all this time writing my memoirs has made me reflect on my life, and I used to get the visions a lot more than I gave myself credit." She flows into a vertical orientation and smiles wistfully. "I miss them, you know?"

I'm not sure I do know what she's talking about.

I've been getting the visions for less than a year, and before I came to Pin Cherry Harbor I was so self-involved that I never gave a second thought to other people's motivations or secrets. I expended all my energy trying to keep my own damaged life under wraps.

An ethereal hand pats my back. "I'm sorry, sweetie. I keep forgetting how bad things were for you. I wish I'd broken the rules sooner and brought you up to live with me when—well, when I was still alive."

The warm feeling of her compassionate energy on my back reminds me of all the love I lacked. "What do we always say, Grams? All of our choices brought us to this point, right?"

She nods as tears stream down her ghostly cheeks.

"As God is my witness, I will get you an after-life hanky if it's the last thing I do." My attempt at humor is met with more tears. "Grams, we can't change the past, but we have so much to be grateful for in the present."

Her trickle of tears turns to a gush of salty sobs. "I don't deserve you."

My arms go right through her insubstantial body as I struggle to comfort her. "What? You don't deserve me? I don't deserve you! Everything you and Silas did to keep your spirit on this side of the veil—"

"Reow." A dose of furry agreement. Pyewacket's confirmation brings the gentle relief of laughter to both of us and we wipe our tears.

"Bottom line, Grams. We literally have the best of both worlds. I'm the luckiest girl and you're the luckiest ghost. Now, let me get some sleep before my big adventure tomorrow and we'll get back to cracking this case after my love life gets a boost."

Grams flashes her eyebrows and shimmies her designer-gown-clad shoulders. "A boost, eh? Is that what the kids are calling it these days?"

I squeal with laughter and toss a pillow at her misty apparition. "Good night, she-devil!"

"Good night, hussy!"

She vanishes through the wall and I collapse onto my four-poster bed, surrounded by the scent of freshly laundered sheets and the warmth of a grandmother's love.

Wednesday morning dawns with all the promise of a classic John Hughes film. My blackout shades roll back to reveal a cornflower-blue sky festooned with cotton-puff clouds. For a moment, I almost break into song, but then I remember that I sing like a caterwauling tomcat.

"Thank heaven for small favors." Grams giggles

and scratches Pyewacket's soft, buttermilk belly as he stretches to life beside me.

"Ree-oow." Despite his relaxed pose, Pye manages to utter a brief warning.

"Come on, you spoiled thing. I'll get your Fruity Puffs while Grams burns herself out trying to choose my Chez Osprey outfit."

She claps her ghostly hands together with glee. "I have so many ideas!"

As the bookcase door slides open, I toss a few facts in her general direction. "Keep in mind that whatever you choose will have to travel in a backpack and unpack wrinkle-free this evening."

She tosses back her head with a haughty flourish. "Fashionistas like me aren't afraid of a challenge."

"Oh brother."

While Pye devours his breakfast, I sneak a few of his sacred Puffs from a safe distance and wander back up to my swanky apartment to see what fate awaits. I'm licking some sugary yumminess from my fingers as the door slides open.

"What in *The Devil Wears*—"

Grams blasts through the wall of the closet and her eyes are positively possessed. "Isn't it amazing!"

"Amazing? It looks like Fashion Week exploded on my bed!"

She swirls around the piles and mumbles strange words that must be for her ears only.

"I said it has to fit in a backpack, remember? We can definitely rule out anything in a full-length gown." My eyes scan across the sea of Swarovski crystals, sequins, and beads.

She zips back and forth between the closet and the bed as though she's Ms. Pac-Man gobbling up designer gowns instead of cherries.

I throw my hands in the air and walk toward the bathroom mumbling. "I liked it better when you couldn't pick things up. At least I could slow you down by pretending I didn't know what you were talking about."

She bursts through the wall like a terrifying attraction in a haunted house and I scream, but thankfully avoid any pants accidents.

"I knew you were stonewalling me! I knew it."

"Look, Grams, I love you and I can never thank you enough for leaving all of this to me, but I want to focus on spending an entire day with Erick, not on whether I'll have to manage six-inch hooker heels on a stone walkway at dinner."

"Hooker heels! Well, I never!"

I tilt my head in a warning. "Oh, Myrtle Isadora Johnson Linder Duncan Willamet Rogers, I think we both know you did. At least five times!"

She tosses a hand towel at me, and I race out of the bathroom screaming and giggling.

We chase playfully around the apartment until I fall onto my couture-clad bed in a heap of happy exhaustion.

"You're crushing the Kors!"

For some reason this sends me into a fresh fit of giggles. As I push myself off the bed of dresses, however, the Kors does catch my eye. "This actually looks perfect."

Grams circles around me with an appraising eye. "The coral would look wonderful with your hair and the ribbed stretch-fabric will hug your curves in all the right places . . ."

I hold the dress to my chest. "Do we have a deal? And can you pretty please pair it with a reasonable heel?"

She arches a perfectly drawn brow. "On one condition."

My gulp echoes in my own ears. "Which is?"

"That you promise to wear that sweet black-and-white camisole with your jeans and not one of your sassy T-shirts."

"They're snarky not sassy, but you have a deal."

We shake hands, or rather hand and ghost limb, and I return to the task of beautifying myself while Grams hums around the place as if I promised to wear eyeliner.

"Don't knock it, young lady. It gives the eye a real boost."

"Get out of my head, woman."

Snickers trail into the closet.

BING. BONG. BING.

We cry in unison, "He's here!"

One last glance in the mirror reflects a look I can live with. I hurry into the closet and grab my backpack, stuff in the dress and the two-inch white kitten heels, and smash the plaster medallion.

Grams waves and blows me a kiss as the bookcase slides open.

CHAPTER 13

By the time I reach the metal door to the alley, my heart is fluttering like a swarm of monarchs returning to Mexico.

Pyewacket stalks around the corner just as the heavy door swings open. "Re-oow."

Erick kneels and holds out a hand. "Was that a hello, buddy?"

Pye glances at the proffered limb, drops onto his backside, and begins his intensive cleaning regimen.

"I thought he was starting to like me." Erick sighs as he gets to his feet.

"You should be flattered. At least he offered you a lukewarm greeting. He only ever hissed at Ror—" I clap a hand over my own mouth and shake my head. "Nope. I'm pleased to never have to say that name again."

"Ditto." He reaches a hand toward my back-pack and I twist away. His eyes widen with shock. "What? I was going to carry it to the car for you."

Flushing with embarrassment, I slip the bag off my shoulder and hand it to him. "Sorry. Instinct. It's the only thing I have from my—you know —childhood."

His eyes fill with tenderness and he cradles the backpack as though it's a newborn. "I'll handle it with care."

And now my tummy is tingly and my heart is a gooey mess.

I can't exactly say I'm happy to get into Erick's patrol car, but it is a relief to be in the front seat for a change. "Why do you drive the sheriff's vehicle when you're off duty?"

"Funny story. We found that when deputies drive their vehicles home they actually take better care of the cars, and the vehicles last longer. Plus, when they park them in their driveways or on their streets, it serves as a deterrent in their neigh-borhoods."

"Thanks, Hick-ipedia." I laugh at my own joke, while Erick shakes his head and grins. As we drive toward the marina, a random thought pops into my head. "So, how does a small-town local sheriff afford his own boat?"

Erick nods in acknowledgment of my question

and his expression turns serious. "I don't have a boat."

I turn toward him and tilt my head. "You do realize what island means, right? The only way to get to Fish Hawk *Island* is on a boat."

He leans back and taps his thumb on the steering wheel. "So, the great Mitzy Moon doesn't know everything."

"Spill it, copper."

"Your dad said I could borrow his boat."

My mouth hangs open for a full twenty seconds before I can formulate a response. "What? Since when are you and my dad boat buddies?"

A hearty chuckle delays Erick's response. "Boat buddies, nice. Actually, I've been helping Jacob make some connections to get the Restorative Justice Foundation off the ground. He said he appreciated me donating my time and offered to lend me the boat anytime I wanted. When I explained what I had planned, he told me where to find the keys."

"I didn't realize you were such a smooth wheeler and dealer. And how is it fair that my dad gets to know your plan when I don't even know the plan?"

"Well, you know we're going to dinner." A half smirk tugs the corner of Erick's mouth up in an inviting way.

"Yeah, dinner. It's ten o'clock in the morning.

Clearly, I'm going to be forced to endure several hours of some kind of nature hike before dinner."

"Ouch. I never took you for a tree hater, Moon."

I slump back against the seat and cross my arms. "Better not be mosquitoes out there."

Erick turns into the marina and parks his cruiser. "Oh, there will definitely be plenty of skeeters, but I've got bug spray. I'd like to say I thought of just about everything."

Exiting the vehicle, I shut the door and rub my exposed arms as a sharp breeze knifes through the thin fog drifting over the great lake, heavy with the smell of damp earth. "Did you bring me a jacket?"

He opens the trunk, slips his arms through a large backpack, carefully picks up my baby backpack, and hands me his brown, polyester-shell sheriff's coat.

"You want me to wear this?"

He nods once.

I slip it on and look at the two empty eyelets where the badge should be. "Do I get the badge, Harper?"

Erick shakes his head firmly. "Never. I hope the world never has to endure that."

I follow him down the steps to the wide dock and recognize the *Tax Sea-vasion* bobbing lightly on the waves. I didn't have the pleasure of meeting my

Grampa Cal, but he clearly had a sense of humor I would've admired.

Erick hops aboard and offers me a hand. He may not own a boat, but he certainly knows his way around one. Within minutes, he's cast off and the engines are puttering away as we navigate to the open sea.

I know it's just a lake, but when you can't see the other shore, it feels like a sea.

"Do you need any sunscreen?"

Smiling, I nod appreciatively. "Actually, yes."

Erick reaches into one of the many pockets on his large backpack, extracts a bottle of SPF 30, and tosses it to me. "Here ya go."

Temporarily slipping out of the jacket, I apply liberally as per the instructions, and, not trusting my own ability to "toss," I lean across and push the bottle back into the side pocket.

Fish Hawk Island wavers on the horizon like a mirage and my tummy flip-flops with excitement. I'm pleased to report no motion sickness on this trip. My first excursion across this massive body of water left me green and nauseous. But I've finally found my sea-legs, which is quite a feat for a desert girl.

Erick expertly berths the boat beside the dock, throws the bumpers over the side, and ties us off. He extracts a smaller day-pack from inside his large backpack and sets it on the planks.

"You need anything from your backpack?" he asks.

I think for a moment and shake my head. "Nope, just my change of clothes in there."

He nods. "10— Copy that."

I chuckle at his attempt to use my vernacular, but at the same time it's kind of adorable.

He helps me out of the boat and we walk up the steps toward an impressive split-rock entrance punctuated by thick pine double doors.

Before he can reach the handle, the door opens and a young man dressed like Daniel Boone, complete with raccoon-tail cap, waves us inside. "Welcome to Chez Osprey. The finest vittles in the north. Are you joining us for brunch?"

Putting a polite hand over my mouth, I hide my amusement while Erick ascertains the location of the owner.

When we reach the stables behind the restaurant, the familiar face of Nimkii appears behind one of the stall doors.

"Sheriff Harper, good to see you, sir. You said you'd be needing two horses today, correct?"

"That's right. Thanks."

Nimkii strides the length of the stable and grabs the reins of two horses, which appear to have been ready and waiting for us. His long salt-and-pepper braid swings rhythmically as he walks.

As soon as the sunlight hits their coats, I recognize the large chestnut mare with a flowing mane and a spirited gate as Cranberry, and the smaller, more subdued roan gelding with short dark spikes of hair down its neck as my buddy Starlight.

I immediately walk toward the roan. "Hi, Starlight. Do you remember me?" I scratch his neck and he whinnies and nods.

Erick laughs and turns to Nimkii. "She talks to her cat, too."

"You need a map?" Nimkii asks.

"No, Cranberry and I know the trail well. We should be back for dinner around seven. Do we need a reservation?"

Nimkii's stoic face breaks into a bemused smile. "For you, never. We'll take care of you whenever you arrive. Enjoy your day, Mitzy."

"Thank you. I sincerely hope today is better than my previous visits to the island." I widen my eyes and exhale.

Nimkii nods solemnly. "As do I."

Erick spots me while I clumsily claw my way into the saddle. And then he easily whips onto the back of his own horse with the expertise of a Wild West gunslinger.

"Lead the way on the mystery tour, Harper."

His shoulders shake with laughter and he clicks his tongue to get his horse on the move.

As soon as Chez Osprey is out of sight, we take a sharp right turn. Now I'm definitely headed to a part of the island I haven't explored. The path is well-worn but the forest is thick, and the dappled green sunlight that fights through the canopy creates a mystical vibe as it reveals pockets of wildflowers. It almost feels as though I've been transported to another world.

Before long, we come upon a break in the trees and Erick calls his mount to a halt. He jumps off and swirls the reins around a low tree limb. He holds my horse while I dismount and ties it up in a similar fashion.

We walk into the meadow and he shows me all the blueberry plants that will be ripe with fruit by early August. Once he finds an open space, he stamps down the long grass and pulls a classic checkered blanket from his day-pack.

"Have a seat, Moon. I'll set up our lunch."

Boy, oh boy, this guy knows the way to my heart. It's food! Yes, the chivalry is not a bad add on, but the direct route—is food.

His pack contains delicious ham and cheese sandwiches, coleslaw, salt-and-vinegar potato chips, bottles of water, a split of champagne, and brownies with fresh strawberries and whipped cream for dessert. If we were scoring this presentation on a scale of one to ten, Sheriff Too-Hot-To-Handle just scored a twenty.

The warm sun and the delicious food make me a little sleepy.

Erick glances over and smiles. "Are you gonna need a nap?"

"I'm sure I can rally. But just a note, if you want a gal to be high energy, you need to provide her with dark chocolate and coffee, not delicious brownies and champagne."

He snickers as he packs up the meal. "You ready to get back on the horses?"

"Yeah, Sundance, I'm ready."

He exhales loudly. "If you're going to make Wild West references, I definitely prefer that you compare me to a famous sheriff like Wyatt Earp, rather than a notorious outlaw."

"Copy that."

Back on the trail, the trees thicken and the elevation increases. I notice fewer birch trees and more varieties of pine as we climb. When we reach the crest of the incline my breath catches in my throat. As though my horse can read my mind, he comes to a stop. "It's breathtaking."

A proud smile curves Erick's lovely mouth. "You see the lighthouse out at the end of that rocky point?"

I nod.

"That's our destination."

I stare for a moment as massive waves crash against the rocks and white foam sprays nearly as high as the lighthouse itself. "Is it safe? I feel like if we walk out on those rocks we will literally be washed out to sea."

"We're not going to the rocks, we're going inside the lighthouse."

"Isn't it locked?"

A secretive grin touches his cheeks. "Guess who has the key?"

I shake my head and laugh. "Would it be the county sheriff?"

He nods and pats his pocket.

The horses pick their way expertly down the narrow rocky path to the lighthouse. The closer we get, the more amazed I am by the scenery. Huge granite boulders and chunks of schist litter the shore of the island. It's almost as though a giant broke the island from a larger piece of stone and those crumbs fell into the lake. The lighthouse seems to increase in size as we approach. If I had to estimate, I'd say it stretches higher into the air than my bookshop, so possibly four stories high. Which means those waves . . . I can't even.

Erick stops the horses a couple of football fields' distance from the lighthouse. There's actually a small wooden shelter with a railing that seems designed for this exact purpose. The horses will be secure, out of the sun, and protected from the wild waves.

He throws the day-pack over one shoulder and helps me down from the back of my horse.

As we navigate the trail to the lighthouse, he slips his hand in mine and every cell in my body does a little dance. We reach the base of the massive structure and Erick attempts to unlock the door.

It takes a few tries and a little wiggling, but that's probably expected in this harsh environment. Inside the lighthouse there's a small desk in the middle of the circular space and a propane heater on the floor next to an uncomfortable-looking wooden chair. There's age and a cool dampness in the air. The wind buffeting the tower howls and whistles in a way that almost sounds like a greeting.

"There used to be a guy that lived out here full-time, but with technological advances they've been able to automate most of the functions, and they just send a park ranger out here to run a quality control check once a month during the summer and quarterly in the off-season." He walks to the base of the winding staircase and gestures for me to follow. "Come on, I'll show you the view from the top."

As we climb the serpentine staircase my excitement gets a boost from each step. However, by the time we reach the halfway point, I'm a little less excited about circular stairs and a little more excited about getting to the top. Truthfully, I'm kind of over stairs at this point.

Erick stops and looks back. "You okay, Moon? You need me to carry you?"

The heat that swirls in my belly at the suggestion of him carrying me is quickly replaced by my manufactured indignation. "As if. I can handle a few stairs, I may not be in 'sheriff shape,' but I can manage to walk. Thanks anyway."

He chuckles under his breath and resumes the climb.

I'd like to say it wasn't worth it, but when we open the trap door, climb into the pinnacle, and gaze out over the greatest lake I've ever seen, my breath catches in my throat and tears come to my eyes. "It's so beautiful." I can't manage to say anything else. I'm too busy blinking back my emotions and trying to prevent myself from causing a scene.

Erick slips an arm around my waist and pulls me close. "I've never brought anyone else up here."

My old friend snark works wonders to staunch my surge of feelings. "Good to know, Harper."

He gives me a little squeeze. "I just didn't want you to think this was my 'go-to' move. Like, I just bring all the girls up here, you know."

I pull away teasingly. "Oh, so where do you bring all the girls?"

"Touché, as you would say, Moon." He pulls me close and I let my breathing fall into rhythm with his.

I don't know how much time passes. I'm lost in the moment, the emotion, the view . . .

Erick turns toward me and his other arm encircles me. "So, what do you think? Did I make a good plan?"

I let him pull me snug against his chest. I tilt my head back so I can look up into his gorgeous blue-grey eyes and admire the reflection of the sky and the clouds. "You make the best plans."

He leans toward me and I close my eyes. The feeling of the sun on my skin and his lips on mine create a sense-memory I will never forget. In fact, I may have to count this as our first kiss. This is what I'd always imagined—this is what I dreamed about.

He pulls away and runs his thumb across my cheek. "Where did you go?"

"What do you mean?"

He shrugs. "Well, not to be this guy, but at the beginning of that kiss it felt like you were into it, but then you drifted off somewhere."

I tilt my head down to avoid the honest intensity of his gaze. "Yeah, that's on me. It's a whole mind-movie thing. Please don't make me explain."

He hugs me tight and laughs. "As long as it

wasn't something I did, you can wander around in your mind all you want."

"Thanks." I hug him back and turn to take another look at the magnificent panorama.

He loosens his hold, and my skin feels cool in the absence of his embrace.

I watch as he circles toward a small cupboard opposite the trapdoor and pulls out two folding stools.

He brings them over, sets them up, and offers one to me.

I happily take the seat.

He fishes around in his day-pack and produces a pair of binoculars. "If you follow the rocks straight back on the right-hand side, you should see an osprey nest teetering in the tops of those huge, dead, white pine trees."

I grab the binoculars and eagerly search the shoreline. It's not as easy as it sounds, but after several unsuccessful attempts, I spot an enormous bird launching from one of the treetops. "*Wild Kingdom*! The wingspan is unbelievable!"

Erick sighs happily. "They're amazing birds. I often wonder what it would be like to fly, and more specifically, to fly as an osprey."

Tracking the bird's powerful flight through the binoculars, I breathe out my admiration. "Pure freedom. Intense power. It looks glorious."

The majestic bird dives like a rocket toward the water and his talons grip a fish. As it returns toward the trees, it appears to bobble the catch.

"It looks like he might drop it!"

"Nah, they have highly adept talons and even special spikes on the underside of their feet that help them hold slippery fish. He's just turning the fish, head into the wind, to make it more aerodynamic."

I turn and stare at Erick as though he's insane. "You're totally pulling one over on the Arizona girl, aren't you?"

His handsome face turns serious. "I swear on my badge."

We wile away the hours watching fish, geese, deer, and even some playful otters. And, of course, Erick shares a plethora of snacks from his impressive pack.

As the sun sinks low on the horizon, he helps me climb through the trap door to the ladder and back down the winding staircase. "Next time we'll drive out on a four-wheeler and bring sleeping bags so we can stay for the sunset and not have to worry about the horses."

I struggle to hide my eager surprise. Sleeping bags? Overnight? I can't even allow myself to entertain the dreamy images pushing at the edges of my consciousness. If I do, I'm sure my knees will buckle and I'll swoon right here and now. I manage to choke out a single word. "Cool."

When he turns to lock the door on the lighthouse, a strange sadness grips my heart and I touch his shoulder gently. "I've never experienced anything like today. Thank you."

He pulls me into a hug and kisses the top of my head. "The first of many, Moon. Count on it."

For the second time today, I find myself blinking back tears and struggling to cage my emotions. A brisk walk back to the horses definitely helps.

On the return journey to Chez Osprey, Erick picks up the pace and I'm forced to dig deep into my elementary-school equestrian memories to stay in the saddle.

While he retrieves our bags from the boat, I wait on the lovely wrought-iron bench below the giant pine tree, where I once sat with my father while I calmed my seasickness after my first trip across the lake.

He opts to change below deck on the boat, while I pop into the ladies' to dress for dinner.

By the time I walk out of the restroom, Erick's hair is freshly slicked back and he's dressed in a suit and tie, waiting in the lobby.

I smile and he reaches for my hand.

He smells all citrus and woodsy, with a hint of

sunshine. His eyes follow my coral-covered curves. "You look amazing in that—" he gulps "—color." An adorable blush rushes up his cheeks and he looks everywhere except at me.

The hostess, in full Native American garb, escorts us to our table. The dinner selections are even better than I remember, and I have to compliment Nimkii on the entirely new and even more delicious menu.

After acorn-flour biscuits topped with fresh wild strawberries and cream, we return to the docks under a star-laden sky.

Our trek toward the marina takes a meandering route. Erick alternates between methodical progress and floating silently under the diamond-studded velvet sky.

CHAPTER 14

WHEN THE EARLY morning light bursts through my unshaded windows, I fear the magical trip to the lighthouse and the unforgettable boat ride under the stars was all a dream.

Grams swirls down like a guardian angel and whispers, "Two things, dear: you're still in your dress from last night, and you talked about your date—non-stop—the entire night. So I can assure you it wasn't a dream, but it definitely sounded amazing."

Sitting up, I grab at the dress, rub the sleep from my eyes, and yawn loudly. "I slept like the dead!"

"Mitzy!"

"Oops. I mean, like a lazy, spoiled fur baby."

"Ree-ooow!" His back arches in an unfriendly pose.

Laughing sleepily, I head into my closet to change for breakfast. "Dearest Isadora, were you, by any chance, eavesdropping when Erick dropped me off?"

"I'm sure I have no idea what you're talking about, young lady." Her innocence reeks of falsehood.

"All right. I might've agreed to meet him for breakfast, but my dopamine levels were flying so high I can barely remember how I got upstairs last night. Did I happen to mention anything about breakfast in my *sleep*?"

Her translucent brow attempts to crease. "Now that you mention it, you may have mumbled something about Myrtle's at 9:00."

Grabbing my phone, I squeak when I see the time is 8:50. "Yikes! Two minutes to walk there. That leaves eight minutes to whip this into shape." I rip the dress over my head as I run to the bathroom to do something with my face. "Clear a path people —or ghosts!"

In the end, I manage to splash some cold water on my skin, apply lip tint, and select the perfect T-shirt, "Running late is my cardio." At least Erick will get a chuckle out of my tardiness.

As I push through the door of the diner, his inviting grin welcomes me and I nearly forget to wave to my favorite chef. But the smell of coffee brewing and lovely breakfast-y things frying warms my heart.

Odell gives me the standard spatula salute, and the ever-efficient Tally places my coffee on the table as I slide into the booth.

"Mornin', Mitzy." Her flame-red bun bobs in my direction.

"Mornin' to you, and thanks for this." I raise my mug in a toast.

She giggles and scurries off to attend to the other locals.

Erick smiles, points to my tee, and chuckles. "How did you sleep?"

Remembering my earlier blunders, I go with the widely accepted expression, "Like a baby." However, I spare Erick my internal debate regarding the reality of babies waking constantly, screaming to be fed, and not actually sleeping.

He gives a friendly nod as Odell slides our breakfasts onto the table.

"How'd you like that lighthouse, Mitzy?"

I point from Erick to Odell. "You told him the plan too? Did everyone in Pin Cherry Harbor, besides me, know *the plan*?"

The boys enjoy a chuckle at my expense.

"It was only fair that I tell Odell. He's the one who showed me that place when I was a kid."

Odell nods his utilitarian grey buzz-cut. "That's

right. My buddy DeVine used to live out there . . . Before the tech upgrade."

I watch the friendly, comfortable exchange between these two important men in my life and a piece of the puzzle drops into place. Erick grew up without a father, but he didn't grow up without a mentor. Sweet, warm happiness fills my heart as a pulse from my bespelled mood ring hums on my left hand. A quick glance shows a much younger Odell pointing to the osprey nests, and a young boy with Erick's intelligent blue eyes eagerly pressing his face against the glass of the lighthouse windows. "Well, it was amazing. Thanks for sharing it with me—both of you."

Odell raps his knuckles twice on the silver-flecked white Formica and walks back to the kitchen.

Time to swing for left field. "How's the investigation going? Do you really think Grant is guilty?"

"There are a few layers, you know. Technically he did kill Edmund, but there's zero motive." Erick drums his fingers on the table. "I just can't help but feel like we're missing something."

I like that he said "we." Even though he could be referring to himself and the other deputies, I'll pretend he meant me. "One thing that keeps bothering me is Butch calling in sick."

"Why? People get sick."

Nodding, I reply, "Sure. Sure. But the Faire is only in town for seven weekends, and I'm sure Butch only gets paid when he rides. You'd have to be nearly on your deathbed to skip out on one-seventh of your income, right?"

Erick leans back and rests an arm on the back of the booth.

Old habits die hard, and my eyes dart downward in case there's a peek of those abs I'm curious to see.

He pretends to ignore my not-so-sly move. "I'll see if Paulsen followed up on that. You make a good point."

Suddenly remembering my other hot tip, I gulp down the home fries I'm chewing and wipe the corner of my mouth. "Hey, what about that sugar glass?"

Erick stares across the table with a full mouth and a raised eyebrow. He points to his mouth as he chews.

All I see are his yummy looking lips, with a little bit of syrup on the edge, that I suddenly have the urge to lick. I flush with embarrassment at the thought and blast him with my additional details.

"So the thing about sugar glass is, it's kind of a skill. I worked on this one film where we needed sugar glass beer bottles for a bar-fight scene, so I ordered a case of twelve. When they arrived, six of them were already broken. Getting the strength of that glass just right, so that it would hold that unique dome shape, remain intact while the lance was being stored in the tack room, but then break successfully on impact—harder than it looks."

"So your point is . . ."

"My point is, who made the glass case for this spike? Whoever made it and fitted it onto the lance, that's your murderer. Everything else can be explained away. Not knowing about the sword, not knowing the spike was meant to be used as a weapon, not intending the spike to be used as a weapon, all of that can sort of be excused. But the person who made that sugar glass dome used it to conceal a murder weapon. Would you not agree?"

Erick spits a little bit of his coffee back into his mug, wipes his mouth, and chuckle/chokes into his napkin. "Is it just me, or is that an unanswerable question?"

I have to join his laughter. "Right? The phrasing of that question has always bugged me. I'm not even sure how or why I put it that way myself, but you're one hundred percent right. What I meant to say was, do you agree?"

"In theory, yes." He crosses his arms over his broad chest and takes a deep breath. "Why don't you go ask your buddy Quince Knudsen what he knows about sugar glass and Birch County?"

"Why Quince?"

"You and I both know that young man is about the only person as snoopy as you. The paper has run stories on everything from gubernatorial races to pin cherry pie contest winners to new statuary in Esther Franklin's garden. If there's ever been a story about sugar glass in Birch County, Quince Knudsen or his dad will know."

I nod. "I seriously hope I don't have to ask his dad. That guy literally has no idea what the word brevity means."

Erick laughs and nods. "He was the journalism teacher and the advisor to the school paper when I went to Pin Cherry High. I swear, he never even made one point per class. Me and my buddies ran an 8 x 8 box pool on whether or not he would remember to give us an assignment. I gotta say, four days out of five, and some days five out of five, he never got around to it."

I lean forward and tap my finger on the table. "So you're telling me that the current sheriff of Birch County formally ran an illegal betting ring at the local high school?" I lean back and smirk. "You're lucky there's no 'film at 11:00,' Harper."

"And you're lucky juvenile records are sealed, Moon."

My mouth makes a silent "O," and I busily straighten the jam packets in their caddy, like it's my job. I knew I was going to regret mentioning my colorful past to him. Finishing my last swig of coffee, I slide out of the booth. "I better see if I can track down Quince."

Erick grins. "You'll let me know what you find out?"

"Of course."

He's powerless to hide his amusement. "In a timely fashion?"

"Always."

"Mmhmm." He shakes his head.

"And you'll let me know what Paulsen says about Butch?"

"Do I honestly have any choice?"

Leaning into the booth, I whisper, "I can be very persuasive, Sheriff."

I wave goodbye to Odell, and Erick's chuckles follow me out of the diner.

CHAPTER 15

THE *PIN CHERRY HARBOR POST* is one of the most ordinary looking buildings in town, but as soon as I enter the old brick structure, I can smell the ink. It reminds me of my bookshop, but in a raw, straight-to-the-source kind of way. There's no one at the birch-clad reception area and, despite a sign encouraging me to ring the bell, my concern that the bell could summon the elder Knudsen prevents me from doing anything of the kind.

I slip into the back room and hear music thumping on the other side of the black cylindrical door that leads to the darkroom. Walking over, I knock on the tube. "Quince, you in there?"

A few moments later the music stops and I step back to give him ample room for his exit. As I've learned on previous occasions, this young high-school boy is not especially comfortable in close proximity to women.

He stumbles out, smelling of chemical baths, with his usual look of disinterest. "Dude, what's up?"

This is what I have come to consider a verbose greeting from the talented photographer who works at both his father's paper and at his high school's gazette. "Got a job for you."

This news bulletin brings a grin to his face. "How much?"

"Don't you want to know what the job is before you agree on a price?"

He shrugs.

"You're slipping, dude." I allow myself to fall into the parlance of his peers. When in Rome . . . "Hey, aren't you supposed to be in school?"

"Graduated last Thursday."

"Good for you. College?"

"Not likely. Not exactly printing money around here." He gestures to the dilapidated office chair and the computer from a bygone era.

Note to self: Set up another scholarship fund at the local high school, for photojournalism, and make sure the inaugural award goes to Quince. It's been a while since I've made any grand phil-anthropic gestures through the Duncan-Moon Foundation. With all this kid's talent, I know a scholarship won't go to waste. "So, I need any information you have on somebody with expertise in sugar glass."

He plops down in the rolly chair in front of his computer as though his legs are made of Twizzlers, spins around once, and holds out his hand. "Hundred bucks."

"Looks like *somebody's* printing money."

He chuckles as I pull some cash from my pocket and hand over the requested fee.

He eagerly grabs the bills. "You want Mr. Kirsch."

"Seriously? You just charged me a hundred dollars for information you already possessed? You didn't even do any research."

His face is a portrait of boredom. "Not like you knew."

"Touché." I turn to leave, but realize I do need a little bit more information. "Where am I going to find Mr. Kirsch?"

"He teaches theater at the high school."

"Hey, you better not be pulling my leg. It's a little hard to believe that a high-school drama teacher has the skill necessary to manufacture complicated sugar-glass items."

"Dude, check out his office."

"Cool. Will do. Pleasure doing business with you." I chuckle as I leave and hear Quince flipping through the bills and mumbling "sweet" behind me.

If it's only the first week after graduation, technically the school should still be open. For a short while I was persona non grata on the school grounds, but a generous donation from the Duncan-Moon Foundation cleared up any misunderstanding, and Principal Puig and I are now the best of friends. I guess I'll see what a hundred bucks bought me.

When I pull the 300SL into the school parking lot an unsettling stew of memories sends my stomach into swirls. Not memories from this particular school, although mistakes were made. These memories are from the long list of schools I attended while in the foster system. Yeah, I got into some fights. Yeah, I usually ran with the wrong crowd. Yeah, I have some regrets. But, at the time, I was coping with the loss of my mother and the difficulties of being an extra person in a variety of families, and, in the grand scope of society, a marginalized human in general. It's not an excuse; it's just what happened. I shake my head to clear the nostalgic fog, adjust my beanie in a way that I hope screams eccentric heiress, rather than rap star wannabe, and exit the car.

Inside the glass-enclosed front office, I tap my toe on a grey carpet square and marvel at the sheer quantity of squares it must've taken to cover all the hallways and classrooms in such an uninspiring color.

A woman bearing the nametag "Donna Jo – Secretary" returns to her post and asks, "Can I help you?"

I can't say I've ever before met a woman whose tone is in such perfect juxtaposition to her words. "I certainly hope so," I gush. "I'm here to see Mr. Kirsch." Trust me, you don't need to be a psychic to predict her next question.

"Do you have an appointment?"

I lean on the counter and soak up her disdain. "I'm sure if you let him know that Mitzy Moon is here to review his program for a possible donation from the Duncan-Moon Foundation, he'll find the time to see me." I'm not a fan of needlessly throwing my pocketbook around, but this woman brings out my catty side. No offense, Pyewacket.

She grumbles something inaudible and picks up the receiver from her desk phone. "Mr. Kirsch, do you have time to see Mitzy Moon from the Duncan-Moon Foundation?" Her eyes track up to my face while she waits for his reply.

I smile in that airline attendant way that clearly is nothing more than a facial twitch meant to disguise their frustration with attempting to serve food at thirty thousand feet.

"What about your prep hour?" chastises Donna Jo. "But— Well, she doesn't have an appointment. Yes. Fine."

Based on the side of the conversation I'm hearing, it sounds like my making an enormous donation to the school last year and setting up a science scholarship is something Mr. Kirsch hasn't forgotten.

Donna Jo hangs up the phone with a tad more force than absolutely necessary and passes me the visitor log. "Sign here." She lays a Visitor badge on the counter. "Wear this at all times and return it to the front office when you leave."

I sign my name with a flourish, pick up the badge, and wink as I leave the room. You and I both know that the likelihood of me returning this badge is about one in—never.

"You need to put that badge on," she calls after me.

I have no idea where I'm going, but I'm eager to escape her presence, so I rush around the corner before stopping to pin on my placard. A student wanders out of a classroom and I stop her for directions. "Hey, where's Mr. Kirsch's room?"

"Behind the theater."

"And the theater is . . ."

The girl points. "Down there. Like, you'll walk right into it."

"Thanks."

She continues on without a backward glance.

Oh, to be a blissfully unaware teen. Although, I honestly don't remember ever being in that kind of daze. I was always on edge, always waiting for something to go wrong or someone to let me down.

The hallway actually does run directly into the theater. The seating is indoor "open air" and makes an impressive un-walled statement in the center of the campus. I walk down a side aisle, between the rows of padded red seats, and mount the steps to the stage.

For a second, I'm gripped with a memory of my one attempt at acting in a junior-high play. That night was the moment I knew I wanted to be behind the camera—not in front. Who knows what would've happened if I'd finished film school. Maybe I'd be working for some big studio in Hollywood.

Not likely.

One thing is for sure, I wouldn't be investigating a murder in a small town in almost-Canada!

I push behind the curtain and find the exit from the backstage area that smells of paint and puberty. Across the hall there's a classroom and a small sign next to the door that says, "Mr. Kirsch." The door is propped open with a brown rubber doorstop, so I walk in.

A surprisingly youthful voice rings out, "The detention room is two doors down."

Apparently, I've still got it. And by "it," I mean, I look like trouble. I search the classroom for the source of the missive. "Mr. Kirsch? I'm Mitzy Moon. I apologize for the getup, I came straight from—"

"Ms. Moon!" A mostly bald head, decorated with wisps of grey-white, pops up from behind a giant candy-bar cutout.

"Mr. Kirsch?"

He strides toward me with the force of a rhinoceros and swallows my hand in a double-handed greeting. "So good of you to consider our program. These kids put their heart and soul into these productions and budgets aren't what they used to be. We're mounting a production of *Willy Wonka and the Chocolate Factory* this fall and I'm forced to cut corners and make do with the efforts of the handful of boys and girls in the summer-school program."

He seems entirely capable of continuing this monologue indefinitely, so I tear my eyes away from his tangle of nose hair and take the opportunity to "check out his office," as Quince instructed.

The plethora of bric-a-brac tucked in every nook and cranny is overwhelming, but as I study it shelf by shelf, a theme emerges.

Sugar glass.

As if on cue, my mood ring burns on my left hand and a quick glance at the stone reveals an image of the silver shards in the dirt of the jousting arena. Now for a subtle transition. "What would it take to bring the production up to your standards?"

Silence.

I'm honestly not even sure what he was saying when I blurted out my question, but it feels safe to assume he never expected such an easy sell. "Mr. Kirsch? What would a healthy budget for this production look like?"

His tiny white mustache twitches left and right.

I step closer and raise one eyebrow expectantly.

"I have notes," he blurts and disappears behind a human-size puff of faux cotton candy. A moment later he returns with a three-ring binder.

Sitting on the edge of a desk, I watch as he flips through the binder, finger tracing down page after page, until finally a hesitant smile lifts one corner of his mouth.

"I'm afraid it would take nearly five thousand dollars to build all of the sets and purchase the special effects lighting package." His shoulders droop and he lays his tome on another empty desk.

I nod approvingly. "Sounds good. Let's call it seven thousand and you can offer ten percent of ticket sales to the animal shelter on opening weekend. Deal?"

His eyes widen and he covers his mouth with one hand.

"Do we have a deal, Mr. Kirsch?"

He nods mutely, but steps forward and shakes my hand so vigorously I fear my wrist may dislocate.

I delicately extract my hand. "May I ask a favor?"

"Of course, anything. We can dedicate the production to you or present you with roses on opening night—"

"No, no. I prefer to keep the donation anonymous. My lawyer will take care of the details and make sure the funds are properly earmarked for your program."

"Certainly. Thank you."

"What I need is a tiny bit of information. I'm told you're an expert in sugar glass, and you certainly have some impressive items."

His body language completely changes, but not in the way I had expected. His features soften, and the manic energy that had gripped him drains away to reveal his true appreciation for the art of theater. "Ms. Moon, I had no idea you knew my secret passion." He approaches one of the low shelves in the office area adjacent to his classroom. Picking up a beautifully crafted miniature mirror with a gilded frame and claw-foot stand, he strides across the room and hands it to me. "I made three of these, that were six feet tall and two feet wide, for our production of *Phantom of the Opera.*

Turning the mirror toward me, I examine it carefully. The craftsmanship is remarkable. My reflection is crystal clear, without any distortion. "This is impressive. I've been on a lot of film sets and sugar glass like this—it's nearly impossible to come by." I gently hand the mirror back to him and nod my appreciation.

"Did you have a specific item you wanted me to create for you? A replica? A showpiece?"

I smiled warmly and let my eyes wander back and forth as I pretend to consider my options. The only thing I'm truly considering is his complete lack of guilt. I definitely expected one of my extra senses to pick up on some surprise or concern when I mentioned the sugar glass. Inexplicably, this guy seems genuinely thrilled I brought it up.

"Ms. Moon, was there anything else?"

Oops. Back to the task at hand. "I was actually wondering if you remembered creating a top-notch silver dome?" Now I should see the guilt I was hoping for.

Nope.

His whole face lights up and he clasps his hands together as though I've just told him he won an Academy Award. "Ah! One of my most difficult projects. I had no model, and no reference item for the final purpose. I was simply given dimensions and told that it must be precise in size and look like actual metal. Apparently the entire project was very hush-hush. I'm thinking it may have been for the new Sandra Bullock movie."

I glance down at my utterly room temperature mood ring and receive no assistance. "That must've been quite a test of your skills."

He exhales dramatically. "Oh, it was unbelievable. I must've had seven or eight samples that shattered during testing before I ended up with a couple of successes. It had to be just the right thickness and strength. I'm told there were several scenes where the item would be jostled before the *coup de grâce*, when it had to break. Like I said, one of my most challenging, but also most exciting, projects."

So much for my theory about the person who made the dome being the murderer. This guy couldn't be more innocent. "Your reputation must stretch far and wide, Mr. Kirsch. Who was your point person on this wonderful project?"

I pick up a little hesitancy, but again not for the reasons I expected.

"I'm not sure I should say. You know how these movie people are. They value their privacy."

"I completely understand. Like I said, I spent a lot of time on movie sets." Sure, it's a blatant exaggeration, perhaps even a lie, but I need the name of this guy's client. "I hate to push, but the Duncan-Moon Foundation is very interested in creating relationships with producers, directors, and production companies as we move forward in setting up drama internships for local students." I could barely get that whopper of a fib out of my mouth.

He bubbles with joy and leans toward me as he whispers. "Well, I suppose he wouldn't mind terribly. He's gone to a great deal of effort to reinvent himself, which, of course, I wildly support. He used to be a student of mine. Never got to tread the boards as an actor, but that boy could run a production like nobody's business. He could just hold all the moving parts in his head. It was genuinely stunning."

The hairs on the back of my neck stand on end and my mood ring begins a slow burn. Something in my churning stomach warns me not to look down. "How lucky you were. I have to know the name of this wonderful student."

He exhales with wonder and pride, leans too close, and whispers, "He goes by Rory Bombay."

My blood turns to ice in my veins. Even though every fiber of my being somehow knew what was coming, I'm still unable to move or breathe.

Mr. Kirsch smiles innocently. "Have you heard of him?"

No part of me knows how to answer that question. Heard of him? What do I say? Yes, I sort of dated him, until he tried to control me with black magic and use me as a cover in his illegal land deal/murder scheme. I manage to suck a tiny bit of air into my lungs and say, "No. Sounds fascinating!"

The proud teacher turns to replace his beautiful mirror on the shelf, and I take the opportunity to swallow the bile rising in my throat and shake uncontrollably.

Before he can ask any additional questions, I have to vamoose. "Thank you so much for your time, Mr. Kirsch. I really must be going. As I said, my attorney will be in touch with all the details. I so appreciate your time today."

Somehow, I manage to walk at a normal human pace until I'm two strides outside his door. Then I break into the hardest sprint of my life.

I never ran track, but I'm pretty sure Usain Bolt could not catch me right now. I skid to a halt outside the Mercedes, jump in, and floor it back to the bookshop.

Of course, I call Erick en route. "Erick? Are you sitting down?"

He assures me that after two tours in Afghanistan and six years as a local sheriff, he can handle news of any kind on his feet.

"Rory Bombay is behind the murder."

The deafening silence on the other end of the phone indicates that my overconfident local sheriff was not as prepared for the news as he hoped.

"Erick? Did you hear what I said? Do we have a bad connection?"

He murmurs something about the bookshop before the line goes dead.

Parking next to the store in the little cul-de-sac on Main Street, I run inside and hustle up to the third floor of the museum. "Grams! I'm so glad you're up here. I've got to get you up to speed before Erick gets here."

All of her concentration is focused on holding an old-fashioned fountain pen and writing what I can only imagine are her memoirs. She barely stirs.

"Grams? Did you hear what I said?"

"Just a moment, dear. I'm right in the middle of a very important story."

Dear Lord baby Jesus. That's it! "Is it as important as the news that Rory Bombay is back in town and is the person who's probably responsible for murdering the Lord Mayor?"

The fountain pen hits the floor and a highly agitated ghost zooms straight at me. "What? How? When?"

I nod in a "told you so" kind of way. "Right?"

"Did he hurt you? Is he in this building? I will haunt him into next week!"

"Slow down, Beetlejuice. I don't actually know where he is. I only know that he was the person who ordered that special sugar-glass dome to conceal the spike on the end of the Black Knight's lance."

She clutches a strand of her pearls and mumbles, "That viper."

"Anyway, Erick is on his way over here, and I need you to be scarce. I've slipped up enough in front of him. I've got to have one normal conversation. Understood?"

Grams presses her hands together in a prayerful pose and nods solemnly. "I promise."

"Thanks." I turn, run back down three flights of stairs, and walk into the bookshop in time to hear Twiggy calling my name.

"Mitzy, Erick's here."

CHAPTER 16

BEFORE I HAVE a chance to greet my guest, a tan rocket races past me to steal my thunder.

"Re-oow." A tolerant greeting from the fiendish feline. Pyewacket's actually "not unhappy" to see Erick. There are very few people on the list of humans he tolerates. The sheriff should consider himself lucky.

"Over here." I walk out from between the stacks and smile as I drink in the strong curve of Erick's jaw. Worry mixed with overprotectiveness pours off him like too much cologne in a 1970s disco.

"You saw him? Is he here, in Pin Cherry?" His hands ball up into fists.

"Slow down, cowboy. You hung up before I had a chance to explain."

Erick exhales, and the pinched muscles between his eyebrows relax. "Is this another one of your hunches?"

"My hunches have solved a pretty big stack of cases, so let's not use that tone when we refer to them. However, this is straight from the horse's mouth." I put my hand up to stop Erick from asking the question. "Not Rory's, but his high-school drama teacher."

The crease returns to Erick's brow as he asks, "Mr. Kirsch. How is he involved?"

"The sugar glass." I purse my lips and arch an eyebrow.

A look of shock washes over Erick's face, followed by a quick flash of embarrassment that only my clairsentience detects. "I forgot all about him. That guy used to pick productions for the theater class simply based on what he could make out of sugar glass. Man, that seems like a lifetime ago. I can't believe he's still teaching over there." For a moment Erick's eyes drift off and I have to pull him out of his pool of memories and back into present-day.

"The good news is that the poor man literally had no idea what he was doing. I mean, he knew he was making a sugar-glass dome—he had specifications and measurements—but he had no idea what it was being used for."

Erick's teeth grind together as he clenches his jaw and hisses out the name. "Rory Bombay."

"Ree-OW!" A warning punctuated by a threat.

"Sounds like Pyewacket would agree."

A fraction of the tension evaporates as Erick chuckles. "I've always liked this cat."

Now is not the time for me to point out the number of times he's warned me to keep "that wild animal on a leash," but I'll permit myself a shudder of an eye roll. "All right, there's my buy-in. Now it's time for you to ante up, Sheriff."

Erick ceases his unsuccessful foray into a friendship with Pye and stands. "Ante up? What are we playing?"

"I believe we're playing a game of *Solve the Ren Faire Murder*. I shared my intel, as promised, and now it's your turn. What did Paulsen find out about Butch?"

Erick shakes his head and crosses his arms. "Mitzy, you just told me that a wanted criminal is actively conducting business in my county. I don't have time to get sidetracked with who called in sick for work or why." I'm not sure if he intends his voice to be stern and reprimanding, but that's pretty much how it feels.

"I disagree. I know you hate it when I talk about my hunches, but I honestly have a hunch that there's a connection." My shoulders sag and disappointment creeps into my heart. "You didn't even send Paulsen out to check that guy's story did you?"

Erick uncrosses his arms and steps closer to me. "Let's get something straight. I don't hate a single thing about you. I find your hunches unnerving and oddly accurate, but I could never hate them."

My heart pitter-patters and my cheeks flush.

"And I did send a deputy to question Butch. Turns out, some guy offered him five hundred dollars to call in sick last Saturday."

I'm about to shout a bold "I told you so," but this time Twiggy steps on my line.

She stomps her biker boot and slaps her thigh. "I knew he was faking! Butch would never miss a chance to humiliate Edmund. Ever since Ursulina chose the Lord Mayor over a knight, Butch couldn't stand the guy. He tried to buy out the old partner last year, but Edmund convinced the guy to sell his half of the interest in the Faire to Simon for some reason."

Erick and I both stare at Twiggy in silence. I'm not sure what he's thinking, but I'm attempting to reconcile her short grey pixie-cut, dungarees, and biker boots with the gold-embroidered finery I observed in the Royal court's arena-side box at the joust.

He's the first to find his voice. "Twiggy, you know these Rennies better than anybody. Is that Faire honestly worth killing for?"

Twiggy shakes her head. "They make a profit, but don't misunderstand. There's a lot of overhead, a lot of logistics, and a lot of infighting. Edmund had an unhealthy love of all things Renaissance. That's what kept him in it for so long. Ursulina just loves the attention. If it wasn't for all the admiration and power she wields as the wife of the Lord Mayor, she wouldn't touch a Ren Faire with a ten-foot pike."

Erick rubs his thumb along the sexy stubble on his chin. "So Butch obviously called in sick for the money. But is there more? Paulsen said he acted a little cagey, but then she thinks that about everyone."

An involuntary chuckle erupts from my mouth. I clap a hand over it and widen my eyes in innocence. Did I just get a little peek behind the scenes? Is everything not perfect at the Pin Cherry Harbor sheriff's station? I know Paulsen ran against him for sheriff in the last election, and it was only a hefty donation from my grandmother that allowed Erick to expand his campaign into every corner of the county and seal the deal. Paulsen has definitely never liked me, I'm sure for that very reason, but she always seems to fall in line. No time to ponder office politics. I've got to push my own agenda.

"I have an idea, but I don't think you're gonna like it."

Twiggy and Erick exchange a knowing glance.

"Hey, let me remind both of you, I have a lot of very good ideas. All right?" My psychic senses pick up on a whole heaping helping of hesitation from Erick and an almost gleeful eagerness from Twiggy.

He gestures for me to share my plan. "I'm not saying no. I'm not saying yes."

"We've looked at the Ren Faire from every possible angle. There doesn't seem to be enough money in it for Simon to try to kill off his partner, or Ursulina to kill off her husband, or Grant to randomly kill the Lord Mayor. But that sword . . ."

A flicker of admiration sparks in Erick's eyes. "Durendal."

"If that's the sword that we think it is, and Rory Bombay is the one pulling the strings, then we know exactly what the motivation was to murder the Lord Mayor."

Erick nods and shoves his hands in his pockets. "Let's say I agree. Even if Rory is behind all of this, we don't know where he is. We don't have a single eyewitness that can place him at the Faire, and we don't have a single eyewitness that mentions a mysterious antiquities dealer approaching them about an artifact."

Pacing between the stacks, I let my fingers run along the spines of the book. I can't very well tell Erick about Rory's penchant for dark magick and evil charms. There has to be a way to find the scoundrel, even if he's cloaking himself.

The rhythmic tapping of Twiggy's boot on the carpet lulls me into a momentary trance.

When I reach the end of the row, it feels as though I've walked into an invisible wall. A thick field of energy hits me, my mood ring turns to ice, and a vision reveals exactly how Rory slipped into the Renaissance Faire. "The Executioner!"

Erick and Twiggy step into the other end of the aisle and ask in unison, "Who?"

"The Executioner. When I was working the pickle cart with Joanie he walked by with his macabre band of dog-men and I could feel how scared she was. I stared at the man in the hood and I almost felt like I knew him, but Joanie started talking and distracted me."

As Twiggy and Erick discuss the possibility of my suspicions being correct, I take the opportunity to replay the executioner's procession with my extrasensory enhancements. This time when I look at the man in the hood, Joanie's words do not distract

me, and the piercing green eyes unmistakably iden-
tify our culprit.

"It's him. I know it's him."

Erick shrugs and sighs. "I can put out a BOLO,
but I'm sure we all remember how well that worked
last time."

Swallowing with difficulty, I walk toward the
sheriff. "We know what he wants. We have what he
wants. The best thing we can do is announce that
the murder has been solved and set a trap."

He shakes his head. "I don't want to put Grant
in that position. I honestly feel like he's the most
innocent person in this whole web of lies. But I
don't want to pretend he's free and get his
hopes up."

"He's innocent. I'm sure we can prove that. But
Ursulina is not. Remember how badly she wanted
to get her hands on the Lord Mayor's possessions?
I'm telling you there's something there. If we can
get a story in the paper about her arrest . . . I can
take care of that part."

Erick scoffs. "Yeah. You and Quince speak the
same language."

"Listen, this will work. We'll announce that
Grant is returning to play the Black Knight and has
been found innocent of all charges, while Ursulina
is being held for questioning as it relates to felony
murder, or something. Then we mention that you're

going to ride in the Lord Mayor's honor and carry his personal sword."

Erick's mouth drops open. "Me? I told you I auditioned to be a knight back in high school. I got unhorsed in the first pass. This will never work."

"You're the sheriff. You're about to let Grant out of jail on good faith. I'm sure he can manage to throw a joust to pay you back."

Twiggy claps her hands. "She's on to something, Sheriff. If Ursulina is some kind of accomplice, putting her in jail will mess up their plan. And if that slimy, underhanded— If 'you know who' wants to get his mitts on that sword, he'll be there."

"This sounds dangerous, Mitzy. I've sworn to protect the citizens of this county, and using one as bait, while possibly endangering an arena full of spectators, hardly seems like an appropriate use of my power."

"Bringing Rory Bombay to justice is exactly what your constituents want. And you're not using one of the citizens as bait. You're the bait."

He throws his hands up in the air. "Oh, that's so much better."

"I promise this will work, Erick. Unfortunately, I know how that self-serving man's mind works. If he set out to get the sword, he's not going to stop until he gets it." I shiver involuntarily.

After several more minutes of debate, despite his reservations, Erick agrees.

Queen Twiggy stomps off to make the necessary calls regarding Erick riding in the joust on Saturday, and Erick drives away to pick up Ursulina and bring her in for questioning.

The balance of the details, bribes, and sword-related enticements are left to me.

CHAPTER 17

WHEN I WALK into the back room at the *Pin Cherry Harbor Post*, Quince doesn't flinch.

"Dude."

"You don't look at all surprised to see me."

"Scanner." He points to the low-tech device next to his ancient computer. "Gonna arrest the wife."

"And that made you think of me?"

"Doesn't add up."

"Well, you and I are here to make sure that everything adds up on tomorrow's front page." I don't even count the bills this time. I just pull out a wad of cash and offer it to him.

He shakes his head and his hands remain in his pockets.

"What's going on? Am I getting *Punk'd* right now?"

Quince's face is deadpan. "What's *Punk'd?*"

"It's the 'cool kids' *Candid Camera*." I wave his question away. "Never mind my weird subreference. Why won't you take any money?"

"Journalistic integrity."

My mouth hangs open. I'm not sure what shocks me more, the multi-syllabic words coming out of his mouth or the concept that this little bribe-taker has a line he won't cross. "So, if I understand you correctly, information and images are for sale, but you draw the line at monetarily influenced stories on the front page."

"Correct."

"Respect." I thump my chest a couple times with my fist, like the world's most unlikely gangster. "Any questions about the photos or the story? Which you will write of your own free will and without undue influence?"

"Nope. Grant's release. Ursulina in custody. The sword—above the fold."

"No sword. We're going to have to leave that securely hidden away until just before the Faire. The last thing we need is to have the sword disappearing before it serves its purpose."

Quince shakes his head. "No sword, no sale."

I point to the wad of cash in my hand and ask, "What? You said no to the money."

"Not gonna waste my time."

"What do you mean, waste your time?"

"No sword, no hype. Locals don't care about Rennies. A priceless ancient sword? That sells papers."

Just when you think you know someone! Not only does this kid have a possible shred of journalistic integrity, he genuinely cares about his father's paper. "All right. Let me make a phone call."

I step outside and ring my alchemist-attorney. "Good afternoon, Silas. I need to ask a favor."

After a lengthy back and forth regarding the weaknesses of my plan and the dangers of alerting Rory to the sword's whereabouts before the big joust, he agrees to a few photographs, with a load of conditions.

Quince is not at all happy to hear that he'll be blindfolded to and from the photo shoot. But when I let him know he'll get to ride in my Mercedes 300SL, he relents.

He grabs his gear and we load up in my vehicle, where he allows me to put a film-changing bag over his head. I know it sounds bad, but it's only a light-proof bag that's used to change out rolls of film in the field without exposing them and ruining the images. It'll work as an effective barrier against him tracking the location of the sword, and it's the only handy thing we have lying around.

I check the security of his makeshift blindfold several times on the way out to Silas Willoughby's home. When he fails to grab the hundred-dollar bill I hold in front of his face, I have to believe he truly can't see where we're going.

Taking the secret turnoff, I arrive at the back of the house and pull into Silas's garage.

Still blindfolded, Quince allows me to lead him through the home to the library.

Silas has the sword laid out for us on a sturdy-legged oak table.

The vault is closed and hidden behind its bookcase.

I wait for an "all clear" signal from Silas. He nods, and I remove Quince's blindfold.

The young man glances around the room and exhales in admiration. "This place is lit."

"I will assume that is a compliment, Quincy. I hope you understand the necessity of secrecy. Please take your photos quickly, but carefully."

Quincy "Quince" Knudsen dives into action, and what he lacks in conversational skills he makes up for with his cinematographer's eye for composition and lighting. He adjusts the placement of the sword, creating depth through highlight and shadow. He snaps off a multitude of angled photographs that cleverly show the sword while obscuring the surroundings. Finally, he steps back, exhales, and nods to me.

"Thank you, Silas." I slip the film-changing bag back over Quince's head and we return to my car.

Once we're back in Pin Cherry, I reach over and pull the bag off the boy's head. "Thanks for being such a good sport about everything."

"Dude. I've wanted to see the inside of that guy's house my whole life."

I chuckle. "It's pretty spectacular, right? But, for the record, I can neither confirm nor deny whether that location is the home of Silas Willoughby."

Quince nods. "You think that sword's the real deal?"

"I do." Part of me wishes I could tell him why and how I can be so certain, but I don't need my gifts to be the next front-page article.

We discuss the details of the story, and he promises to make the article an irresistible invitation.

My phone buzzes. A text from Erick informs me that he's "Bringing Ursulina in. ETA 5." I slow down in front of the newspaper office, but make a U-turn. "I'm assuming you've got more film."

Quince grins and pats his camera case.

"I'll drop you off at the end of the block. I don't

think it makes the right statement for me to arrive with you."

He chuckles. "I got this."

As he exits the vehicle, I offer my thanks.

He bobs his chin. "Dude."

Overall, I'm shocked by the volume of words that escaped from the normally succinct lad, but the classic "dude" never fails to amuse.

I've seen enough of Quince Knudsen's moving images to know that with him a picture truly is worth a thousand words. No matter what the story says, he'll make sure that the images on the front page of tomorrow's paper send a clear invitation to Rory Bombay.

CHAPTER 18

AND NOW FOR the part of my plan that holds the most promise. I pack an overnight bag and drive back to Mr. Willoughby's strange Gothic mansion. Later this evening, the one and only Sheriff Erick Harper will join me. In the morning, we'll remove the sword from the vault and drive out to the Renaissance Faire to prepare for the joust. Simple, right?

Let's hope.

When I return to the manor, Silas has prepared the tea tray, with a selection of nearly unpronounceable loose teas, a delicious mound of scones, and what appears to be homemade wild strawberry jam.

We take our tea in the sun room, and afterward

he gives me a guided tour of his culinary and medicinal herb garden while we wait for Erick to arrive.

My attention wanders during the tour and my brain is already on to the next topic. "Is there a path down to the water?"

Initially, he harrumphs at my lack of appreciation for his botanical knowledge, but then a cagey grin appears. "Is there?"

And I believe we're about to have yet another lesson. "Whenever you answer my questions with another question, I know you think I'm supposed to already know the answer. But I don't. I've only been here once, technically twice, and I've never been to the shore. So, can you just tell me if there's a path?"

"It would be far more beneficial for your education if you were to use your gifts to obtain the information that you seek."

I throw my hands up in a gesture of surrender. "And what must I do to obtain this information?"

He smooths his bushy grey mustache before he answers. "When you pose a query, the respondent cannot help but hold the answer in their mind. Whether they verbalize the answer or not, that is a choice. Yet that moment when the answer manifests within them—that they cannot control. Your gifts allow you to snatch that moment from the ether. Ask me the question again, and allow yourself to take the answer from its resting place."

I roll my head back and forth in frustration, not looking forward to disappointing my mentor. "Silas, is there a path on your property that leads down to the shoreline?"

The moment the words leave my mouth, I sense the answer in his mind. There's a gate, covered by a curtain of ivy, and a winding staircase descending into the rock face. "It's true! I mean, if what I saw is true, then, it's true. I saw a gate hidden behind some ivy and steps going down into the rocks."

Silas smiles like a proud parent. "It is true. Can you locate this gate from the information you received?"

"Probably, but I better grab another scone for sustenance, in case I get lost."

His chuckling jostles his hang-dog jowls and he nods his approval.

I pop into the sun room, grab a pastry, and search the backyard for the swath of ivy from my vision.

And there it is. Clear as day. Amazing.

Thick folds of the creeping plant nearly obscure the gate. But as I lift them aside, I discover the latch is in good working order.

Pushing through the gate, I let it close quietly behind.

The narrow stairs begin almost immediately. With one hand sliding along the cool rocks for balance, I wind my way down the cliffside to a small inlet. A narrow strip of sand leads into a cave-like area where a small boat is moored to a thick cement pylon.

Much like the gate's latch, the boat seems well cared for. I follow the curve of the rocks, sit on the natural stone platform, and listen to the waves crashing against the rocky cliff walls beyond this peaceful little cove.

With my limited maritime experience, I lack the confidence to take such a small vessel onto such a great lake. Still, I've heard stories about the occasional dead calm that grips the water, and I can picture myself rolling along the contours of the shore under those circumstances.

A light tingling touches my left hand and I glance down at the smoky cabochon of my mood ring and see the Birch County Sheriff's logo slide by on the door of a cruiser.

Jumping to my feet, I smack my head against the low ceiling and stifle my cry of pain as I shout, "Erick's here!" My voice echoes eerily off the rounded surfaces in the damp recesses of the cavern.

The journey back up the winding staircase is not nearly as exciting as the descent. I'm reminded of the hatred of stairs that gripped me at the lighthouse. If not for the brisk breeze gusting across the open water, I would be dripping with sweat by the time I reach the gate.

Carefully passing under the thick vines of ivy, I hurry back to the house and call out to Silas. "Is Erick here?"

There's no reply, but faint voices are coming from the direction of the library. As I near the entrance, Erick's question reaches my ear.

"What makes you so sure it is Durendal?"

A spike of fear lodges itself in my back and I'm unable to take a deep breath. My entire story about Silas's weaponry expertise is about to go straight out the window!

I creep closer, careful to stay near the edge of the hallway where I'm hoping a creaking board is less likely to be found.

Silas clears his throat and replies, "Weaponry of that era contains several distinct markers."

He goes on and on with inane details about sigils, metallurgy, patinas, embellishments . . . It legitimately sounds as though Silas knows what he's talking about. Thankfully, it looks like any hint of my vision-assisted provenance is safe, for now.

As I enter the library, Erick turns and smiles enticingly.

Silas smooths his mustache. "Of course, the museum will confirm the sword's provenance before it is placed in the permanent collection. But it is our duty to protect it from theft. It has obviously languished in private collections for centuries and deserves prominent display."

Erick absently nods in agreement as he walks toward me. "And where have you been?"

"I walked down to a—little beach with—a boat." I stumble over my words, not sure if the path I've taken is supposed to be a secret.

Silas nods in my direction and picks up the story. "There is a staircase carved into the rocks that leads down to a protected cove where I store my boat."

Erick nods. "That must be quite a staircase. Did you build it yourself?"

Silas's heavy jowls rise as he smiles. "I did. It took me ten years, but it was a labor of love."

Erick and I stand with rapt attention, expecting the story to continue. It does not.

Instead, Silas ushers us out of the library and promises to have dinner on the table in half an hour.

"Would either of you care for an aperitif?"

Erick gives me a little wink. "That sounds divine."

I'm barely able to contain my giggles. I know he used the word just to poke fun at me, but I appreciate a good call back as much as the next guy. "Yes, thank you."

Silas shuffles over to a small countertop above a

decoratively carved cupboard, opens two massive doors, and reveals an impressively stocked bar.

"Wow. That's quite a collection."

He nods as he retrieves miniature stemware and an interesting bottle, dressed in plaid and capped by a large cork.

He pours a small amount of the ruby-red liquid into each of three small glasses. The stems are no longer than my pinky finger, and the bowls are etched with intricate starburst patterns.

Handing a glass to each of us, he picks up his own and offers a toast. "To your success tomorrow."

Erick and I raise our glasses in response and reply, almost in unison, "To our success."

I down the liquid in one gulp and feel a warm tingle spread through my abdomen. "That's delicious. What is it?"

Silas slowly savors his polite sip and I realize my mistake too late. Clearly, lowbrow Mitzy Moon is used to more of a "shots" kind of consumption, whereas our ever-cultured host views this as a sipping situation.

"It is a cranberry liqueur, which is bottled in the region."

Quickly sliding my hand up to hide my empty liqueur glass, I nod my appreciation. "Well, it's good. Thank you."

"Would you care for a refill?"

Looks like I'm busted. Attempting to protect what's left of my dignity, I place my free hand over the top of the empty glass. "It's probably best if I don't head down that road."

Erick grins and tilts his head with interest. "And what road would that be?"

"It's gonna be a dead-end road for you, Buddy," I playfully reply. "We should focus on reviewing the plan, enjoying what I'm sure will be a wonderful dinner, and getting a good night's sleep."

Silas raises his tiny glass. "I'll drink to that." Finishing his cranberry aperitif, he excuses himself to lay the table.

Erick meanders along the curved wall of the library and inspects rows of books lining the built-in cases. "Are you much of a reader?"

"Um, I own a bookstore."

He continues to run his finger across the titles. "I know. Obviously, I know. What I'm asking is, do you like books? It's not like the bookstore was your thing. You inherited it from your grandmother. You could sell it and move anywhere in the world you wanted."

"I'd never sell the bookstore. I can't sell the bookstore to anyone. Why would I even want to sell the bookstore?" My heart is pounding in my chest.

Erick turns around slowly, concern pinching his

features. "Did I touch a nerve? I wasn't implying that you should sell the bookstore—"

"No. Of course not. Sorry, I guess you did touch a nerve." The anxious energy coursing through my veins sends me on my own circuitous route through the library.

Time for some classic misdirection. "There are some amazing titles in this collection." The hairs on the back of my neck tingle just a moment before Erick slips up behind me and puts a comforting arm around my waist.

"You didn't answer my question, Mitzy."

"Hmmm? Didn't I?"

"You didn't. What are you not telling me about books and the reading of them?"

A lump rises in my throat and the room seems to shrink around me. "It's— my mom."

"You used to read with your mom?"

"She read to me every night. I loved books. I loved the sound of her voice sending me off to dreamland. In the months before she—passed away, she was working so hard. I can't even remember how many jobs, and some nights I had to read to her. Afterward, I would read to myself—and hear her voice in my head. But it faded—"

Erick circles his arms around me and looks down with such intense compassion that the lump in my throat threatens to break loose and release a flood of tears.

I blink hard and look away. "I drowned all the pain under a flood of movies and television shows. Books brought back too many memories."

He pushes the hair back from my face and smiles. "Maybe we can ease back into it. I'd be happy to read you to sleep sometime, Moon."

The way he says my last name breaks the tension and I let myself melt into the firm planes of his chest. "Thank you. I'd like that."

CHAPTER 19

THE MORNING of our carefully planned sting dawns shrouded in fog. I've seen some foggy days since my arrival in Pin Cherry Harbor, but this is the pea-soup fog of legend. This is John Carpenter's *Fog*.

As I look out my second-floor window, I can't even see to the edge of the property. The low rock wall bordering the back yard is invisible. It feels like an ominous sign and I rub desperately on my mood ring, begging for a message.

"Come on ya moody thing. Give me a sign!"

There's a light knock at my door and I hope I wasn't overheard. Luckily, I somehow slept in my jeans and T-shirt so there's no need to scamper around in that classic movie scene when the leading lady searches for a flimsy robe to pull over her revealing pajamas.

Walking toward the door, I brace myself for the probable cancellation of my plan. "Good morning."

Erick's hair is a damp tousled mess and I am shocked to absolute speechlessness when my eyes wander down to discover him wearing only a towel. The abs that have been the ambition of my visual explorations are displayed in all their glory.

Yes, I'm speechless. If this is a sign, thank you precious magic ring!

"Morning, Moon. Just wanted to let you know the bathroom is free."

Words come out of my mouth. "Here thanks, sure good." Sadly those words make no sense!

Erick raises an eyebrow and chuckles. "Guess you're not much of a morning person."

I attempt to lean casually against the doorjamb, but my hand slips and I knock my head against the decorative wood trim.

He's quick to catch me and keep me upright. "Maybe you should eat something before you get in the shower. I don't want you slipping and falling in that claw-footed bathtub/shower operation and cracking your skull open."

All I can manage at this point is a clumsy nod. I close my door and lean against it, desperate to get air into my lungs. Joke's on him. I wasn't planning on taking a shower this morning.

Wiping the sleep from the corners of my eyes, I hurry downstairs to find Silas while Erick is sadly covering those breathtaking abs. Unfortunate, but if I'm going to get anything done today I'm sure we both agree it's for the best.

"Silas? Silas are you down here?"

"In the dining room."

I stumble toward the sound of his voice, not sure which one is the keeping room, which one is the larder, or which one is the dining room. But, lucky for me, my hearing is quite good.

"Good morning, Mizithra."

"Morning. What's the deal with this fog? I've never seen fog like this. Should we call off the whole thing?"

Silas actually has to put a hand on his plump little belly as he chuckles away my foolishness. "My dear Mitzy. This is typical June weather in Pin Cherry Harbor. By 10:00 a.m. this fog will be nothing but a distant memory and we will be staring at the packed bleachers around the jousting arena."

"We? You're going to go to the Renaissance Faire with us? I don't remember this part of the plan."

"It is in the sword's best interest if I keep it in

my sight at all times."

Shrugging, I mumble, "Fine with me." I rub my hands together eagerly. "Now, how about that breakfast?"

"Follow me." He leads me into the kitchen and points to the coffee service tray, while he scoops up a second tray filled with breakfast-y deliciousness.

"Oh, before I forget. I need you to set up a journalism scholarship at the high school and award the first one to Quince. And can you also make a seven-thousand-dollar anonymous donation to the theater department."

"Would this be damage repair or a bribe?" Silas smooths his mustache and narrows his gaze.

"Neither. This time I'm legitimately doing it from the goodness of my heart."

Silas lifts his mug and mumbles, "Will wonders never cease."

Before I can retort, Erick saunters into the kitchen in a plain white T-shirt, snug in all the right places, and a casual pair of slim-fit athletic pants.

"Is that what you're wearing?"

His eyes widen and he scoffs. "Ouch."

I wave my hands rapidly to dismiss his feigned injury. "I didn't mean it like that. I just thought you'd wear your uniform."

"My uniform? Underneath a suit of armor? I don't think so." He pats a pocket on the fancy sweatpants. "I got my badge. When it comes time to take down Rory Bombay, I'll be ready."

I give a low whistle and flash my eyebrows. "Pride cometh before the fall, Sheriff."

His expression turns serious and he leans away. "It kinda sounds like you want me to fail."

Before I can reply, Silas steps in. "Enough you two. We must take proper sustenance to prepare for our day. You must be on your guard. You must take nothing for granted. And you must expect the utterly unexpected where this fiendish purloiner is concerned."

Erick and I exchange a gaze of unspoken truce and power through the scrambled eggs, pancakes, and Canadian bacon. Which I suppose in Canada is just called bacon. However, I've never been.

As I help Silas clear up the morning dishes, he makes an announcement. "Mitzy, you should proceed to get changed. You'll ride in front with Erick, and I'll ride in the back with the sword."

Erick looks at me questioningly.

"Silas will be joining us as the sword's protector."

To Erick's credit he makes absolutely no joke. He nods appreciatively. "Do you need any help getting the sword to the patrol car?"

Silas stands completely still and looks sternly at the sheriff. "I do not."

Hurrying upstairs, I change into my wench-wear, tie on my mask, and forgo the elf ears. I honestly forgot to pack my spirit gum, and today surely won't be about my costume.

Erick and I anxiously wait in the cruiser while Silas retrieves the sword.

When he steps into the garage, my eyes widen and I silently grip Erick's knee. "You see it too, right?"

His breath comes in short strained puffs and he whispers, "Yep."

The ever-proper Silas Willoughby is dressed, head to toe, in Renaissance garb. His balding head is topped with an intricately embroidered round cap featuring a turned up hem, edged in gold lace. He wears a brocade waistcoat with a ruffle-sleeved shirt poking out and a small ruff around his neck. And if all of that is not enough, he has donned knee breeches and woolen hose.

I'm speechless and struggle to contain the laughter bubbling in my throat. However, the sight of the holy relic, Durendal, in his hands, sends shivers racing across my skin and erases all humor. It takes all the control I barely possess to keep the visions from surging in and overwhelming me.

Silas climbs into the back of the cruiser and lays the sword reverently across his lap. "Let the games begin, Sheriff."

Festival Friday does not disappoint! The patrons' entrance to the Faire already has two lines of cars backed up for nearly a mile on the main road. Fortunately we're in the sheriff's car, so we hit the lights, dive into the verge, and speed past everyone. I feel like a princess.

Turning into the parking lot, I'm surprised to see five additional Birch County Sheriff's vehicles and one Lake County Sheriff's vehicle.

"You brought in deputies from Lake County?"

"We needed the bodies. We've got to cover the exits and run a team through the Faire in hopes of finding the Executioner before the joust. I'd prefer to take Rory into custody in a secluded area, and lessen the exposure of innocent citizens."

And there it is. Our tender moment in the library is a distant memory. Sheriff Harper is back at work and fully in charge of this manhunt.

"I'll run over to the pickle stand and see if Joan has any news. What time should I meet you at the arena?"

"The first joust is at 10:30, but you don't have to come." He reaches a hand across and grips my fingers.

The mood ring on my left hand heats up rapidly and I wonder if he can feel it. He doesn't seem to react. "I'll see you at 10:15."

"You don't have to come. I'd almost prefer if you

didn't."

Silas makes no effort to contain his snickering in the back seat. "It is probably best if you focus on the task at hand, Sheriff. We both possess enough experiential knowledge to assure ourselves that Miss Moon cannot be deterred."

Erick shakes his head. "Fair enough. See you at the joust."

"See you at the joust."

We exit the vehicle, and Erick and Silas pass through the gates ahead of me, veering toward the arena.

I hurry to the pickle cart, hoping that Joan has some useful gossip to share.

She sees me approaching and waves spastically. "Arwen! I wasn't sure if I'd see you today. I thought you might already be at the other cart."

The urge to smack my own forehead with the palm of my hand is nearly irresistible. Having completely forgotten about the second pickle cart, I'll have to squeeze information out of Joan quickly and get to my post. "Oh, I just wanted to say hello before I head over there. Maybe I'll come back and hang out with you during my break."

"Okay. But you better hurry. Gates open in five minutes."

"Sure, I was just wondering—"

"Hey, where are your elf ears?"

This calls for one of my foolproof excuses. "I overslept."

Joan giggles. "Story of my life."

"Anyway, have you seen the Executioner this morning?"

Joan leans her head to the right. "It's so weird that you asked that. He's supposed to be down by the gates. Him and his creepy dog-men harass the patrons as soon as they come in. You know, just to get them in the mood right away. But I saw him about ten minutes before you got here, and he was headed toward the arena. All by himself." She swirls her finger in a circle near her temple indicating that the Executioner's action is crazy.

I don't have the heart to tell her that he's headed exactly where I expected. "That's totally weird. See you later." I jog off in the direction of the second pickle stand, but as soon as I'm out of sight, I double back toward the arena

The opening cannon sounds, and faster than you can say "Huzzah!" the grounds are swarming with people.

Unfortunately, at this exact moment, I cross paths with Lady Natalia. "Well met, Arwen. How are things going with the pickles? Are you all set? Should we expect double the profits today?"

I'm fresh out of excuses, and it must show on my face.

"Everything okay?" She leans toward me with concern.

Ah ha! I can almost see the cartoon lightbulb click on over my head. "I'm so sorry. I've got a little digestive thing this morning. I really have to get to the privy."

She pats me on the back and ushers me past. "I completely understand. No problem. I'll run over and cover the stand for a few minutes. Get back as soon as you can."

Well, there goes my plan to race to the arena and help Erick apprehend our fugitive. Ducking out of sight, I pull the phone out of my dress pocket and send him a quick text. "Executioner on his way to arena."

I wander around for a few minutes—hopefully the right amount of time for a pretend bathroom break—and head back to pickle palace, part two.

"Arwen, thank you for coming back so quickly. I've got to get to the Royal box before the Queen arrives. Good luck!"

Lady Natalia lifts her velvety skirt and races off.

Great. There's already a line, six people deep, in front of the cart.

After a brisk thirty minutes of pickle trade, I close up the cart and direct the remaining patrons to the other location before rushing to the arena.

There are only minutes before the exhibition

starts, and the stands are spilling over with spectators.

Sneaking into the knights' area behind the arena, I search for Erick.

I pass by the stall containing the enormous black stallion, but I don't see Grant. Stopping one of the squires, I ask about the White Knight.

She points to the opposite corner, and I arrive just in time to see Erick's squire strapping him into his borrowed armor. The regular White Knight must be particularly weight-endowed, and the armor hangs around Erick's middle, making him look like a child in a Tin Man costume.

"Hey, you didn't reply to my text."

Silas silently shakes his head and his jowls rub against his ridiculous ruff.

Erick struggles to look over his shoulder. "I don't have my phone. I left it in the cruiser so it wouldn't get broken during the joust."

Stepping closer, I whisper urgently, "Rory is here."

He tugs free of his squire's ministrations. "Where?"

Silas steps closer to Erick and grips the ancient sword tightly.

"Joan said she saw the Executioner headed *away* from the front gates and toward the arena about a half-hour ago."

The Herald rudely steps in front of me. "Sir Knight, the joust begins. Mount up."

The squire tightens the last of the straps on Erick's armor and hands him his helmet.

"Good luck, Sir Knight."

Erick nods absently. "Yeah, thanks."

Silas threads the sword belt around Erick's waist and fastens it tight.

I step closer. "What should we do?"

A harrumph escapes from Silas. "I believe it would be best to keep to the plan."

"Well, according to the *plan*, I have to ride in this joust. And I guess Mitzy better see if one of her hunches can help you two find Rory."

My psychic senses pick up on the fear behind Erick's gruff words, and I know it must be hard for him to do nothing while I potentially put myself in danger. "What if I find him?"

Erick nervously clangs his helmet against his breastplate. "I don't know. Run into the middle of the arena and tear off your mask. That should get my attention."

The more dire the circumstances, the more inappropriate my humor. "There's probably a few other things I could tear off that would get your attention quicker."

Erick's cheeks redden and he exhales. "Oh, man. Good one, Moon."

His squire reappears with the majestic white stallion in tow, and Erick quickly swings into the saddle.

I reach down and tear a strip off the bottom of my dress. "A token of my favor, Sir Knight."

Erick chuckles but ties it around the pommel of his saddle nonetheless.

The thunderous stomping and clapping of the audience send shockwaves throughout the arena, and he nudges his horse into action.

As soon as he leaves, Silas encourages me to attempt to call a vision.

I lean up against the nearest wall and close my eyes. Somewhere in this arena, filled with thousands of people, I need to zero in on the energy of one person. The unsavory task of visualizing Rory Bombay's double-crossing face does not come easily.

As his image wavers in my mind, a sudden crystal-clear picture of Grant materializes instead.

My chest tightens. In my vision, Grant is unconscious. "Something's wrong with Grant."

"Your vision was not of Mr. Bombay?"

"Not even a little."

"You must find Grant. I'll report to the arena and keep an eye on the sword." Silas whisks away like Renaissance nobility.

I abandon my efforts to locate Rory and focus on Grant's energy.

As I move along the row of stalls, my palms tingle and the hairs on the back of my neck stand on end. When I reach the last door, I shove it open and look into the tack room. I'm met with a horrible sight.

Grant, sprawled across the floor with a faint trickle of blood oozing from the back of his head.

Stepping back, I shout at the nearest squire. "Call 911. Grant's in here and he's injured. He needs medical attention right away." As soon as my orders are being followed, I turn and run toward the arena.

One thought stabs mercilessly at my heart.

If Grant is lying on the floor of the tack room, the person wearing the Black Knight's armor can only be—

I race through the gate, run into the middle of the arena, and rip off my leather-and-feather mask.

But I'm too late. The horses are already rocketing toward one another, and the Black Knight's lance is aimed directly at Erick's heart.

Secured over the tip is the second of Mr. Kirsch's two successes, the now-familiar grey glass dome, covering what I know is a deadly spike.

With no thought for my own life, I run straight toward that wooden railing spanning the length of the area, screaming at the top of my lungs, "It's Rory! Rory!" as I gesture madly toward the Black Knight.

The knights are a second from collision and I have no way of knowing if Erick hears me.

I want to close my eyes. I don't want to watch this—but I can't look away.

A bone-splintering clash echoes through the arena and the audience gasps in unison.

The saddle on the white stallion is empty, but Erick isn't lying on the ground.

The Black Knight is galloping around the end of the wooden railing.

Where is Erick? I run forward just as the White Knight pops up from the other side of his mount, where, I guess, he was balancing in the stirrup. What the—?

He rakes the reins across his horse's neck and turns to face the advancing enemy.

But Rory is already on top of him. He slashes at Erick's sword belt, rips the scabbard and Durendal from Erick's waist, and whips his own horse into a run with the reins.

There's no way I can catch up to a racing horse or jump in front of it and hope to spook it into stopping. So I use the only trick I have left. I shout at the top of my lungs, "Where are you going, Rory Bombay?"

And hoping for that nanosecond that he holds the answer in his mind, I focus every ounce of my extrasensory perception.

Yes! I got it!

Ducking under the wooden railing, I shout, "I know where he's going."

Erick spins his mount around and gallops straight at me. At the last minute, he veers slightly right as his left arm scoops me off the ground and hurls me onto the horse behind him.

I'm not sure whether he can hear me or not, but I shout my admiration all the same. "That was some *Man from Snowy River* flare, Harper."

As he presses the horse to a run in pursuit of the Black Knight, he asks, "Where's he going?"

"River. The barge."

The amazingly powerful white stallion is chewing up the ground, but there are two of us on his back, and we don't seem to be gaining on Rory.

"Get this armor off me." Erick twists uncomfortably. "Please."

As I squeeze my knees tightly around the horse, I have to release my arms from Erick's waist. Struggling desperately to undo the straps and buckles that secure his armor would be no easy task standing still, but I'm finding it nearly impossible to accomplish while bouncing around on the back of a horse.

Let's be honest, of all the ways I may or may not have dreamed of undressing the local sheriff, removing his armor on horseback never made an appearance. But I'm determined to succeed, and before long, I've removed everything except the pieces protecting his calves, and his gauntlets.

The river is in sight, and I watch in horror as Rory leaps off his mount, draws Durendal, and slices through the mooring rope of the barge.

"It's still sharp," Erick mumbles in awe.

The Black Knight jumps on board as the flat-bottomed boat slowly moves out into the river.

Luckily it's a low-flow year, and the barge is creeping at a snail's pace.

By the time we race up behind, Erick is already swinging his leg up and over his horse's head. He lands on both feet, ripping off his greaves and sollerets as he runs.

For some reason, known only to him, he leaves his gauntlets on when he jumps into the water. Regardless, his powerful strokes take him to the barge in seconds.

I watch from the banks in helpless terror as Rory swings the sword at Erick. The ancient blade glances off the gauntlet.

Thank heaven for serendipity.

Erick pulls himself onto the boat, rolls clear of a second sword strike, and searches for a weapon.

Rory charges forward.

Erick grabs one of the metal poles holding the Queen's colors at the corner of the canopy and deflects the attack.

While Rory is fighting to kill, it's clear to me that Erick is attempting to protect Durendal.

The barge is near the middle of the river now, and the current is picking up.

Rory loses his balance and stumbles.

Erick ducks low and body checks Rory below the belt.

The fiend buckles forward.

Erick's lightning-fast reflexes wrench the sword from his hand. He puts the tip of Durendal to Rory's neck. I can't quite hear what he says from shore, but listening with all my senses, I'm sure it's something like, "End of the road, Bombay."

Defying all expectation and sanity, Rory turns and dives into the deepest part of the river, still wearing a full suit of armor.

Erick haltingly lowers the sword and gazes toward me.

Lifting my hands in confusion, I shake my head.

"Call for back up," he shouts.

I dial the sheriff's station and tell the deputy I've nicknamed "Furious Monkeys" that the sheriff needs backup at the Renaissance Faire.

He calls out an additional direction. "Tell

Deputy Baird to call the draggers."

Passing along the command, I explain that a fugitive escaped by jumping into the river.

She asks why we need the draggers and not a motorboat.

When I tell her that the fugitive was wearing a suit of armor, the laughter is deafening.

Probably not a good idea to share that part of the exchange with Erick. "She's on it."

He nods, lays the sword down, and picks up one of the long wooden push-poles. As he maneuvers the barge back to shore, his shoulders sag.

"At least you got the sword."

He steps off and makes a new loop from the remaining rope. After securing the barge, he tries to hand me the sword. "You'll make sure Silas gets this in time for his meeting with the museum's curator on Monday?"

My arms hang limp at my sides. I'm in no hurry to touch the powerful relic.

"What's wrong? Why won't you take it?"

Without replying, I walk over to the sweaty steed and remove the torn strip of my dress from the saddle horn. I wrap the fabric around the hilt and carefully grip the sword, without letting my skin touch the metal. "Oils from my fingers."

He chuckles and raises one eyebrow. "If you say so."

Deputy Paulsen arrives, out of breath from her jog across the grounds, and pushes past me to take control of the scene.

Erick immediately briefs her and, as they discuss the "mop up" operation, I turn away, hoping to drift back toward the arena, find Silas, and unload this mysterious weapon.

Imagine my surprise, when I discover that Silas and the entire arena of spectators have come to us.

Clutching the sword in one hand, I wave pitifully with the other. Silas shuffles toward me in full regalia, but his progress is quickly eclipsed by the unladylike rush of an over-eager Joan.

"OMG! Arwen, you're like a freakin' superhero!" She stops a few strides shy of me and narrows her gaze. "Are you an undercover agent?"

A weak half smile lifts one side of my mouth. "Not exactly."

She puts a hand on one hip. "Is that really a wig?"

I shake my head. "Nope."

Silas finally arrives and gently relieves me of the historic artifact.

Joan somehow manages to ignore the spectacle. "Um, what's the deal with that sword?"

I slip an arm around her shoulder and smile. "How 'bout I buy you a turkey legg and tell you the whole story—beginning to end?"

CHAPTER 20

By the time Joan and I return to the scene of the crime, as it were, the pieces of the Black Knight's armor are laid out like the bones of a corpse. However, this is clearly an exoskeleton with no human center. There is a gauntlet, one greave, and a sword belt missing.

But the biggest disappointment of all is that nowhere along the shores of the beautiful river is there a Rory Bombay in handcuffs.

"Give me a minute. I want to ask Erick what they found."

"Yeah, no problem." Joan sinks onto a wooden bench and stares as the draggers continue to dredge the riverbed.

When I walk over to Erick, my clairsentience picks up on the seething rage bubbling just beneath his calm, wet exterior. Struggling to keep from staring at the way his white T-shirt clings to his body, I attempt to cheer him up. "Don't worry, you'll get him next time."

Erick's fists tighten until his knuckles turn white. "That's what we said last time. I'm sick and tired of this guy making a fool of my whole department. The draggers keep saying that I shouldn't worry about it, that he drowned." He shakes his head. "Did you look at that armor? There's something pretty strange about how he got out of it."

"Really? I'll take a look." Walking over to the eerie arrangement of black metal parts on the grassy landing, I immediately see what Erick is talking about. The buckled straps that secure the pieces of armor around the wearer are intact. These pieces weren't removed by unbuckling them. Instead, the rivets that hold the leather straps onto one side of each piece seem to have been melted, causing the straps to release from the anchor point.

I'm certain that alchemy was involved, but there's absolutely no way I can mention my theory to Erick. I scan the crowd for any sign of Silas, but he's nowhere to be seen. He probably left the Faire and returned the sword to the vault at his manor. Can you blame him? Looks like my only option will be to play dumb.

Erick walks over and looks down at the armor.

"What do you think? It looks like it was melted, right? How could he possibly have had a device that could melt rivets underwater?"

"No idea. It's definitely strange."

Erick leans back and narrows his gaze. "It's strange? That's all you have to say? The girl who's full of hunches and unbelievable answers . . . Come on, Moon, I expected more from you."

In my heart, I know he's under a lot of pressure and he doesn't mean to lash out at me, but it still hurts a little. "Hey, I'm just observant. Obviously, I couldn't observe him underwater. I have no idea what he did down there. Maybe they were already melted, and he planned to escape down the river all along? Bottom line is, you recovered the sword. It's a priceless piece of history, and Rory will get what's coming to him sooner or later."

Erick shakes his head. "That's what I'm worried about. Every time this guy slips through my fingers, someone else dies. If he hadn't gotten away last time, the Lord Mayor might still be alive. And what about Grant? I don't have an update on his condition. What if the body count is higher than I imagine?"

"Erick, I know it's your job to keep the county safe, but you're not responsible for Rory's actions. Something snapped inside that man's mind a long time ago, and one day you'll put him away. Today just wasn't that day. I'm sorry."

"I wish I could accept that."

Paulsen marches over and shoves her way into our midst. "Sheriff, they need you down at the station. Ursulina wants to talk."

"She does? Yesterday she wouldn't even confirm the spelling of her name. She swore she'd never tell me a thing. What changed?"

"No idea. Maybe it was going through booking? They collected all her personal effects and gave her a jumpsuit. She probably wants to cut a deal. You know she lawyered up. The guilty always do."

I roll my eyes and wish the world was as simple as Deputy Paulsen thinks it is.

She returns to the edge of the river to shout additional instructions at the draggers.

Erick prepares to leave the scene.

"Hey, Sheriff, can I get a ride back to town?"

He turns and, despite the stress of the situation and the disappointment of losing Rory, smiles warmly and gestures for me to follow him. "I can drop you at the bookstore before I head into the station."

I hurry to catch up to him and link my arm through the crook of his elbow. "Or, I could wait in your office while you interview Ursulina. Would that be all right?"

He chuckles, and some of the tension he's holding in his shoulders drains away. "Sure. You can wait in my *office*."

I squeeze his arm and we pick up the pace back to the cruiser.

Back on Main Street, Erick parks in front of the station and, while he walks to the back to retrieve the prisoner from lockup, I stop to chat up Furious Monkeys.

"So, what level are you?"

Without looking up from her all-encompassing game she replies, "162."

"Wow? Either the levels are getting easier or you're getting a lot better."

She grins and pauses the game. "Getting a lot better." She looks me over top to bottom. "So what's all this?"

"I was working at the Renaissance Faire to get information about the recent murder."

She laughs. "Of course you were." Jerking her thumb over her left shoulder, she asks, "I suppose you'll be waiting in his office?"

I nod appreciatively and push through the crooked wooden gate.

The scratched metal desks in the bullpen are empty. All the deputies are either out on patrol or at the Ren Faire interviewing eyewitnesses. The old wood paneling stretching halfway up the walls once again reminds me of a dash of Sheriff Valenti's HQ from *Roswell*, with a heaping helping of Sheriff Andy Taylor's Mayberry office.

I don't even bother with the ruse of going into Erick's office. I step directly into the observation room between Interrogation Rooms One and Two.

Ursulina looks terrible. Her hair is a mess, her mascara has smeared under her eyes, and "orange jumpsuit" is not her color.

Erick sets up the recording device, presses record, and begins the session.

I flip the silver toggle above the speaker and sit back to *observe*.

"And you're certain you want to proceed without your lawyer present?" he asks.

Ursulina nods immediately.

"I'm sorry, but you'll have to answer verbally." Erick points to the recording device.

"Yes, yes, I'll tell you everything. I don't need my lawyer."

"Let's start with the sword. Did you know it was valuable?"

"No. Not in the beginning. Edmund was obsessed with trashy old stuff. It looked like all the rest of his flea market finds."

"When did you become aware of the sword's value?"

"I got a phone call from an antiques dealer —collector."

"Did this antiques collector give you a name?" Through the one-way glass, I can see the muscles in Erick's jaw flex as he clenches his teeth.

"Yes, Rory Bombay." Her words are angry, but her eyes are filled with pain.

"What happened next?"

"He met with us, midweek, a couple of months ago—between Faires—and offered Edmund a few thousand dollars." Her fingers trace loops on the table and her shoulders droop.

"Why didn't Edmund want to sell the sword?"

She pounds her fist on the metal surface. "Because he was Edmund. Because he never sold anything. He just collected more and more and more things! We have storage lockers in three states! The Faire is barely profitable, and any extra money we make goes into buying his trash and storing it!" Her face is red and her chest is heaving with angry sobs.

"Did Mr. Bombay increase his offer?"

I lean forward in anticipation.

"Sort of."

"What do you mean?"

"He asked me to meet him privately. He said he understood Edmund's attachment, and that he might have a solution that would help both of us."

"And this is when he offered to kill Edmund?"

Erick is eager to get something to link Rory directly to the murder.

Ursulina leans back as though she's been slapped. "What? No. No. He never said he'd kill Edmund! He gave me a present. He said if I could find a way to convince Edmund to sell the sword, he'd make it worth my while."

"And what did he mean by worth your while?"

She shrugs her petite shoulders. "Well, he didn't say, specifically. I just kind of thought it would be more presents and stuff."

"Did you accept his offer?"

She nods.

"Please answer verbally."

"Yes. I accepted his offer. But only to talk to Edmund. I never wanted him dead."

Flicking the silver switch off, I step back. I need to see this gift she mentioned. If I know Rory Bombay, and unfortunately I do, the gift he gave her was charmed in some way. Most likely in a way meant to twist her to his will. I recklessly push the intercom button. "Sheriff Harper, I have some information you need to see right away."

Erick turns and faces the one-way glass. His eyebrow raises. He stops the tape and asks Ursulina to wait for a moment while he gets this new information.

He walks out of the interrogation room and into

the observation room. "Moon, this doesn't look like my office."

I smile innocently. "Whoops. I guess I made a wrong turn."

"Look, it's one thing for me to bend the rules and let you observe the interrogation, but I'm going to have to draw the line at you impersonating an officer."

"I didn't impersonate an officer. I never said I was an officer. I just said there was some information."

Erick throws his hands up helplessly. "Fine. What's the information?"

"Can I see the personal items you collected from her? I'd like to take a look at the item Rory gave her."

"What makes you think it would be with her personal items? Why would you assume she was wearing it?"

"Trust me. She was wearing it."

Erick smiles and his eyes sparkle with mischief. "A hunch?"

"Can confirm."

He opens the door. "Wait in my office. My actual office, this time."

I humbly hustle across the hall and take a seat.

He returns a few moments later and dumps the contents of a large envelope on his desk.

As I reach for the items, he grips my wrist and offers me a pair of latex gloves. "Let's not get your fingerprints on everything."

"Copy that." I slip on the gloves and push the items back and forth with my finger. When my hand nears a large teardrop ruby pendant, surrounded by diamonds, I can feel the wickedness of the charm. I have no idea if Rory was working with the Polish gypsy to enchant this item, or if he has some new source for his dastardly plans, but this item reeks of compulsion. All of my extra senses are firing off red flags. This is definitely one of those things that Silas would tell me not to touch. I make a quick poke at the necklace, and as soon as my finger touches the blood-red stone, I can hear Rory whispering in my ear.

"Come to me. Trust only me. Come to me. Trust—"

Yanking my finger away from the necklace, I shake my head violently to dislodge the horrible come-hither spell. "The necklace. It was the necklace."

Erick scrunches up his face. "What about it?"

"Rory used the necklace to control her—I mean —influence her. That's got to be the reason she agreed to talk to you today, because she's not wearing it."

Erick shakes his head. "What are you talking

about? It's a piece of jewelry. Wait, do you think it's some kind of listening device?"

"In a way. If you ask her, I bet you'll find that Rory may have manipulated her into a compromising situation. And then used that information to blackmail her. I don't think she had any choice but to do what he said."

"You're serious?"

"Deadly serious. Ask her if Rory was blackmailing her."

Erick places the items back in the envelope, presses the clasp flat, and tosses his gloves in the trash bin. "I'm gonna finish the interrogation now. You'll be here when I'm done?"

I nod, and struggle to suppress my grin.

As soon as he returns to Interrogation Room One, I slip across the hall into the observation room.

When he resumes the interrogation, the facts unfold almost exactly as I predicted.

She can't seem to adequately describe how Rory had so much control over her, but having suffered the effects of his manipulative magicks, I know exactly what went wrong.

Fortunately, her explanation about the blackmail satisfies Erick's curiosity and seems to explain her actions. He promises that her cooperation will go a long way toward securing leniency from the DA, and ends the interview.

Standing in the observation room for a moment longer, I can't help but think about Pyewacket and his wedding ring clue . . . that cat is a little spooky. My heart goes out to Ursulina as she weeps for Edmund. Who knows why she originally married a man nearly twice her age, but clearly she never meant to see him dead.

I hurry back into Erick's office and, when he returns, I can see the regret on his face. "What's wrong?"

"She's guilty of cheating on her husband, she's definitely guilty of unwittingly assisting in the planning of the murder, but something tells me without Rory's influence, Edmund would still be alive."

"I have to agree. That man is poison."

Unexpectedly, Erick scoops his arm around my waist and pulls me close. "I'm just glad he didn't poison you."

Smiling up into Erick's admiring blue-grey eyes, I blush with agreement. "Me too."

The ringing of my cell phone in the pocket of my dress causes me to jump back in alarm. "It's Twiggy. I better take it." The information she shares with me is not necessarily good news. "Looks like we have to go back to the Faire tomorrow, Sheriff."

Erick nods. "Sure. I have to finish getting measurements and information for the report, and I'll need to interview some of the squires.

"Sure, but there's more."

"Like what?"

"Apparently, we've been named the Lord and Lady of the Faire, and we will be required to lead the Maypole Dance."

He blanches, and his eyes widen in what can only be described as horror. "What?"

"Queen Twiggy informs me that after we left the Faire today, the Royal Court had an emergency meeting. Due to our heroic actions, they've made a special dispensation to appoint us honorary members, or some nonsense, and give us the pleasure of leading the Maypole Dance."

Erick shakes his head. "I'd hardly call it a pleasure."

I shrug. "Is it bad? Why is there a Maypole Dance in June?"

He sits on the edge of his desk. "They do a Maypole Dance every weekend. It's just one of the celebratory attractions of the Faire. A lot of pomp and circumstance, but I suppose after all the bad publicity it can't hurt to try and lift everyone's spirits and get through one day without any tragedies."

"So we're doing this?"

He stares at me helplessly. "I guess so."

"If we're part of the Royal Court, we're gonna have to up our garb game."

He shakes his head. "You can't be serious."

"The Faire will still be open for a few more hours today. I better head back over to Pendragon's and get us some new costumes for tomorrow." I can barely contain my giggles.

"How do I get myself into these things?" Erick drops his face in his palm and moans.

"Don't worry, my lord, you shall be the grandest dandy at the Faire."

He exhales dramatically. "That's what I'm afraid of."

CHAPTER 21

"GRAMS! I CAN'T BREATHE!" There is something vaguely horror-movie-ish about having a ghost cinch you into a Renaissance costume so tightly that your lungs collapse.

"Oh, Mitzy, you'll be fine. I'm simply helping you to look your best. You don't have to act like I'm trying to kill you." She trusses me up, floats back, and grins maniacally. "Perfect."

The emerald-green hourglass figure, in all its Celtic glory, that stares back at me from the mirror is unrecognizable. Part of that may be because Grams is attempting to convince me to wear this flowing auburn wig with curls trailing beyond my waist.

Regardless of the visual effect, my rib cage feels legitimately cracked, and tiny puffs of air threaten to cause hyperventilation. "Please, just let it out a little."

"When I was your age—"

"I know. I know. You knew ten women who would kill to wear this for five minutes."

"Reeeee-ow." A warning.

"See! Even Pye agrees with me. Now loosen this torture device so I can bend over and fill his bowl, or you know he'll make us both pay."

"Re-ow." Thank you.

"No, thank you, Pye."

"Kids these days." Grams mumbles all sorts of generational slurs as she unties and reties my corset —a fraction looser.

I toss the wig on the bathroom floor and struggle to wrap the forest-green velvet cloak over my shoulders and pin it with the penannular brooch that Chip insisted I "must have."

Translucent tears trickle down Grams' cheeks.

"What's wrong? Don't you like it? Don't be mad about the wig. It's too hot. I swear I'll wear it some other time."

She continues to gaze at me and sniffle.

"You hate it."

"I love it, dear. You're an Irish princess."

"What is it then?"

"I wish I could see you in the Maypole Dance."

"I shall have Queen Twiggy record it on ye olde cell phone."

Grams clutches her pearls and her face glows like a halogen bulb. "Would you?"

I curtsy deeply and nearly fall over. "You have my word, m'ghost."

"You're such a hoot. Now get downstairs and feed Pye before—"

BING. BONG. BING.

"Too late!" I giggle all the way down the spiral staircase, and I'm struggling to catch my breath when I open the big metal door.

Lord Erick is a sight. He is only half dressed and his ruffly shirt is untucked.

"Did you get dressed in a tornado?"

"It's hot. Everything itches, and I can't believe I have to dance in all of this." He gestures to the remainder of his costume in the back seat of the cruiser.

"At least you can breathe." I point to my wicked corset and cringe. "I just have to feed Pye and then we can go." I turn to run to the back room, but he grabs my hand. "What?"

"You look amazing."

My cheeks are probably as red as the long wig Grams wanted me to wear. "Thanks. I feel foolish."

"You don't look foolish. You're—it's—you look good. Did you get all of this at Pendragon's?"

"Oh yeah. Chip was floating three feet off the ground when I left that place. He made a whole season's commission off one sale."

Erick's sexy smile disappears and he nods seriously. "Yeah. I'll pay you back for my stuff."

Oops. I keep forgetting that my inheritance allows me to be more impulsive than most. "No way. I'm the one who decided to go costume crazy, all right? You're not responsible for my retail therapy issues."

He nods and exhales. "Okay, but let's not make a habit of it."

"Understood, my lord."

He laughs. "I'll wait in the car, with the air conditioning on full blast."

"Copy that."

When I step out of the bookstore, and the humidity hits me, I immediately pat myself on the back for my decision to NOT wear a waist-length wig.

It takes a significant amount of maneuvering, complaining, and struggling with skirts to successfully wedge myself into the front of the patrol car.

To Erick's credit, he helps without any judgment.

Once again, we use the benefit of the sheriff's vehicle to allow us to bypass the wait and slip through the back gate unhindered.

"I need to go say 'hello' to Joan. She texted me this morning and made me promise to show her my getup."

"Sounds good. I need to talk to Simon and ask him a few follow-up questions."

I manage to curtsy without falling, and Erick gives a slight bow as he struggles to keep on his plumed hat.

"I shall see you at the Maypole, my lord."

He chuckles, "And I you, my lady."

Joan is absolutely thrilled with my outfit.

"Are you sure?"

"Positive." She grabs a small bag from a cupboard and locks up the pickle cart. "Follow me!"

The large open area where the Maypole is erected has a generous covering of straw on the ground around the pole. Ribbons, two-inches wide, in a plethora of colors, hang from the top of the pole to form a beribboned puddle on the ground.

A beautiful crown of flowers, ivy, and herbs adorns the very tip of the Maypole. Rennies and mundanes are lining up all around the outer edge of the circle, waiting for the dance to begin.

Nineteen girls and nineteen boys are selected from the ring of spectators. The boys approach the pole first, each grabbing the end of a ribbon and stepping out to the perimeter. The girls duck between them, each grabbing a ribbon and stepping halfway between the pole and the circle of boys.

Queen "Twiggy" Elizabeth steps up to the podium. "Lords and ladies of the realm, may I introduce our guests of honor. Lord Erick and Lady Mizithra!" She breaks character for a brief moment to cackle at my expense, and I'm reminded that I pay her with just this sort of entertainment—namely, my occasional humiliation.

The crowd cheers. "Huzzah! Huzzah! Huzzah!"

Two ribbons remain. Erick and I step between the boys and girls, each grabbing our respective ribbon and joining our gender circle.

Queen Twiggy explains the pattern of the dance, but I seem to be the only one listening. Either the rest of the participants have danced the dance before, or they're not that interested in performing it correctly. A small band of Renaissance minstrels kicks off the song and the boys begin rotating clockwise.

The girls move counterclockwise, and I attempt to match the pattern of weaving in and out of the boys in a serpentine motion, like the girl in front of me.

Before long, the laughter takes over and one by one the boys and girls get tangled up and fall to the straw. Eventually there are only six of us remaining.

The speed of the music increases, the speed of our serpentine dance increases, and I'm almost certain I'll be the next to fall.

Remarkably—possibly because the rest of the participants are roughly ten years younger—Erick and I are the last two dancers standing.

We finish the colorful woven pattern, encasing the Maypole, and the crowd chants, "Kiss. Kiss. Kiss."

I blush helplessly, but Erick indulges the audience.

The music continues and the spectators surge into the Maypole circle, everyone dancing and enjoying the day.

As Erick and I move toward the edge of the crowd in search of shade, I notice the injured Grant seated on a large stump under an elm tree.

Before we can fight our way through the crowd to say "hello," Joan appears with a mug of mead and a bottle of water for him. Grant's head is bandaged, his left eye bruised, but other than that he appears none the worse for wear as he takes her hand and gently kisses the fingers.

Up on the dais, with the rest of the Royal Court, Lady Natalia is tapping her toes and clapping her hands. I glance into the shade under a large oak tree, where Simon the blacksmith seems equally moved by the music.

"I'll be right back."

Erick smiles. "Okay. I'm going to go check on Grant."

I thread my way over to Simon and whisper in his ear.

His eyes travel up to the stage where he catches sight of the elegant-but-feisty Lady Natalia. He smiles and blushes adorably.

"Go on. Ask her."

He approaches the edge of the stage and calls out to her.

She smiles and walks over to him.

I wait with bated breath while he asks his question.

Her eyes widen, and she smiles with heartfelt joy as he reaches up to lift her off the stage and escort her to the Maypole.

Now that my good deed is done for the day, I'll see about getting "Ricky" to buy me a mug of mead.

A year ago, I never would've pictured myself enjoying a Renaissance Faire in full regalia. But then, a year ago, I could barely picture myself paying my rent.

Times, they are changing.

Huzzah! Huzzah! Huzzah!

End of Book 7

A NOTE FROM TRIXIE

Huzzah! Another case solved! I'll keep writing them if you keep reading...

The best part of "living" in Pin Cherry Harbor continues to be feedback from my early readers. Thank you to my alpha readers/cheerleaders Angel and Michael. HUGE thanks to my fantastic beta readers who continue to give me extremely useful and honest feedback: Veronica McIntyre, Renee Arthur, and Nadine Peterse-Vrijhof. And big "small town" hugs to the world's best ARC Team – Trixie's Mystery ARC Detectives!

My favorite note from my patient and persevering editor Philip Newey has to be: "I know you are trying to make words look old-worldy, but mcad is already an old word and doesn't have an 'e' [at the end]." Some author's dread edits, but I always look forward to Philip's straightforward, no-nonsense feedback. I would also like to give a long overdue THANK YOU to Brooke, for her tireless proof-reading! Any errors are my own, as my outdated version of Word insists on showing me only what it likes and when it feels so moved.

My love of Renaissance Faires began in Shakopee, Minnesota and followed me across the country, where I now call the Arizona Renaissance Festival home. It's one of my Bucket List items to visit all the faires in the U.S.

Also, quick thanks to Drew for explaining "box pool" betting to me!

I'm currently writing book nine in the Mitzy Moon Mysteries series, and I think I may just live in Pin Cherry Harbor forever. Mitzy, Grams, and Pyewacket got into plenty of trouble in book one, *Fries and Alibis*. But I'd have to say that book three, *Wings and Broken Things*, is when most readers say the series becomes unputdownable.

I hope you'll continue to hang out with us.

Trixie Silvertale (June 2020)

Mitzy Moon Mysteries 8

A flamboyant funeral. A dashing gigolo. Can this psychic sleuth beat the odds on murder?

Mitzy Moon is never one to celebrate death. But a compelling invitation to a 1920s themed memorial service, aboard a riverboat casino, entices her to take a gamble. And the only thing hotter than the tables is the newly wealthy widower —until he disappears.

Despite the extravagant decor, Mitzy smells a rat in designer clothing. And warnings from the sexy sheriff, her meddling Ghost-ma, and a spoiled feline all fall on deaf ears, as the list of greedy suspects grows with every spin of the wheel. She'll have to play her cards just right or end up on a fatal losing streak!

Can Mitzy win against the house, or will she double down on death?

Wakes and High Stakes is the eighth book in the hilarious paranormal cozy mystery series, Mitzy Moon Mysteries. If you like snarky heroines, supernatural intrigue, and a dash of romance, then you'll love Trixie Silvertale's dicey whodunit.

Buy *Wakes and High Stakes* to cash-in on a caper today!

Grab yours here!
readerlinks.com/l/1157801

Once you're in the Club, you'll also be the first to receive updates from Pin Cherry Harbor and access to giveaways, new release announcements, behind-the-scenes secrets, and much more!

THANK YOU!

Trying out a new book is always a risk and I'm thankful that you rolled the dice with Mitzy Moon. If you loved the book, the sweetest thing you can do (*even sweeter than pin cherry pie à la mode*) is to leave a review so that other readers will take a chance on Mitzy and the gang.

Don't feel you have to write a book report. A brief comment like, "Can't wait to read the next book in this series!" will help potential readers make their choice.

★★★★★

Leave a quick review HERE

https://readerlinks.com/l/1075501

★★★★★

Thank you kindly, and I'll see you in Pin Cherry Harbor!

ABOUT THE AUTHOR

Trixie Silvertale grew up reading an endless supply of Lilian Jackson Braun, Hardy Boys, and Nancy Drew novels. She loves the amateur sleuths in cozy mysteries and obsesses about all things paranormal. Those two passions unite in her Mitzy Moon Mysteries, and she's thrilled to write them and share them with you.

When she's not consumed by writing, she bakes to fuel her creative engine and pulls weeds in her herb garden to clear her head (*and sometimes she pulls out her hair, but mostly weeds*).

Greetings are welcome:
trixie@trixiesilvertale.com

 bookbub.com/authors/trixie-silvertale

 facebook.com/TrixieSilvertale

 instagram.com/trixiesilvertale

Made in the USA
Middletown, DE
29 November 2021